Christmas Joys

Good Housekeeping

Christmas Joys

GREAT HOLIDAY RECIPES
and
DECORATING IDEAS

by the Editors of
GOOD HOUSEKEEPING

HEARST BOOKS
New York

Good Housekeeping

EDITOR-IN-CHIEF • ELLEN LEVINE
ART DIRECTOR • SCOTT YARDLEY
LIFESTYLE DIRECTOR • DONNA BULSECO
FOOD DIRECTOR • SUSAN WESTMORELAND

Good Housekeeping Christmas Joys

GUEST EDITORS: RICHARD KOLLATH, ED McCANN
PROJECT EDITOR: MARYANNE BANNON
COVER AND BOOK DESIGN BY: DEBORAH KERNER
WRITER: BLAIR BROWN HOYT
ORNAMENTAL ILLUSTRATIONS BY: RICHARD WAXBERG

The credits and acknowledgments that appear on page 157
are considered to be a part of this copyright page.

Library of Congress Cataloging-in-Publication Data
Good Housekeeping Christmas joys: great holiday recipes
and decorating ideas/
by the editors of Good Housekeeping.
p. cm.
Includes index.
ISBN 0-688-16032-8
1. Christmas cookery. 2. Christmas decorations. 3. Handicraft.
I. Good Housekeeping.
TX739.2.C45G66   1998
641.5'68— dc21   98-15255
                                                         CIP

Printed in the United States of America
First Edition
1 2 3 4 5 6 7 8 9 10
www.williammorrow.com

CONTENTS

FOREWORD

The countdown to the holidays starts early at *Good Housekeeping*—
we're already thinking about the following year soon after New
Year's Day. Preparing for this joyous season is a tradition we cherish and
enjoy—and take seriously. We loved the idea of a book that could help
us do it all—and that is how *Good Housekeeping Christmas Joys* was born.

We know it's not easy to put together a memorable celebration
filled with great food and beautiful decorations. Like you, we're guided
by thoughts of family and love, hallmarks of the *Good Housekeeping*
tradition, and we have a practical bent as well, making lists of
ingredients we need, checking out the prettiest ribbons and wrapping
papers, and sharing ideas for wreaths and table settings with our moms,
friends, and readers.

In my family, it's the classics that are the most rewarding at the
holidays: delicious dishes passed down through the generations, cookies
that are tempting year after year, and ornaments that seem new again
each time they're unwrapped. We hope these pages filled with our
favorite things will become your favorites as well. And let me know
about your family's traditions, with all the trimmings!

In a season filled with joy, I wish you a healthy, fun-filled,
beautiful holiday.

ELLEN LEVINE

INTRODUCTION

The magic of Christmas comes but once a year, with cherished traditions and beloved rituals shared with family and friends. But the planning, decorating, shopping, and cooking sometimes seem just too much to handle. It's always helpful to have guidance when organizing a perfect celebration.

We at *Good Housekeeping* can provide just that in *Christmas Joys*: a magic touch for a traditional celebration updated for today's lifestyle. As you thumb through these pages, you'll see how you can transform your home, inside and out, into an enchanting realm of glinting lights and special decorative touches. We put the perfect holiday in reach with decorating ideas that look lavish but can be accomplished without a lot of time and money. And we give you a range of projects, so that you can create your own customized Christmas. Capture the light and warmth of the Christmas season with our luminaria, softly glowing along a walkway. Illuminate the night with a medley of old-fashioned storm lanterns hanging from tree branches.

Then bring the warmth to your doorway and inside. Welcome friends to your home with a new-fashioned Mixed Greens Wreath scented with lavender and cinnamon sticks; or adorn a window with a radiant White Statice Wreath. Scent the house with bowls of aromatic citrus pomanders or create a diverting detail with a beribboned pomander on a doorknob. For an unexpected decorating idea, we show you how to fit a juice glass with flowers into an old ice skate – easy, but elegant! Or try the woodsy arrangement of sheet moss, dried fruits, and spices (opposite) that can be conjured up in minutes using easy-to-find materials from the supermarket, garden-supply center, and your own backyard.

And, of course, we give you ideas both inspirational and practical for the grand centerpiece of this celebration – the tree. Along with useful tips on selection and care, you'll find instructions for a charming assortment of quick and easy ornaments.

Now that your home sparkles – inside and out – extend that magic to your holiday table with our triple-tested and guaranteed-to-be-irresistible recipes. Party with your guests and tantalize their appetites with Christmas Quesadillas, Lacy Parmesan Crisps, and Caviar Pie. Serve a delectable entree like Pork Crown Roast with Apple Stuffing or Crispy Citrus Goose to a beaming family and guests. Keep time in the kitchen to a minimum with do-ahead side dishes like Sweet Potato and Apple Gratin or Green Beans with Honey-Pecan

Butter. And for the grand finale choose a divinely delicious dessert: perhaps our luscious Tiramisu Cake or a stunning Brandied Bûche de Noël. And for many of us, the best of all: *Christmas Joys* has cookies, cookies, and more cookies – Great Granny's Old-Time Spice Cookies, Peanutty Yummy Bars, Chocolate Sambuca Cookies, Cinnamon Twists, and Jelly Centers, to name a few.

We give you, then, our best wishes, decorating ideas, and recipes, for a holiday season that shimmers and sparkles. *Christmas Joys* will inspire and delight you. You'll think happy thoughts of Christmas and be able to enjoy your holiday season with the greatest of ease.

The TREE

The grand centerpiece of every Christmas celebration is the family tree—steeped in tradition and dressed in festive trimmings. From its selection to its decoration, the tree presents opportunities for family outings, parties, and traditions. For a really fresh tree, check your local area for tree farms where you can pick and cut your own and turn the "chore" into a family outing.

This glorious tree is trimmed in a sparkling fantasy of gold and silver balls accented with gold lamé bows and twinkling white lights.

KNOWING YOUR EVERGREENS

Red Cedar

Blue Spruce

White Spruce

Hemlock

Austrian Pine

Scotch Pine

Western Cedar

When you select your tree or greens for wreaths and garlands, you'll find many varieties from which to choose. The length, color, glossiness, texture, and fragrance of the needles as well as the color and texture of the bark vary from type to type. Let personal preference be your guide; all of the varieties shown here are wonderful.

When you select a tree, consider: Do you want one that's tall and slender? Neat and petite? Grand and stately? In addition to size, shape, and symmetry, consider whether the branches are sturdy enough for ornaments and whether the needles will make placing ornaments awkward or difficult. Of course, you'll want a tree that's fresh and will keep its needles at least three to four weeks. When testing for freshness, bend some branches and needles; they should be pliable and spring back. Or grasp a branch and pull your hand toward the tip. If lots of needles fall off, the tree is too dry. With a smaller tree, hold it upright, and pound its trunk on the ground. Falling needles will tell you to pass it by.

As soon as you get your tree home, saw a half inch off the bottom of the trunk, put the tree in its stand, and immediately add warm water. (Cut trees, like cut flowers, take in warm water more readily than cold.) A tree's sap quickly seals its cut and prevents water from being absorbed.

If you don't plan to decorate right away, set the freshly cut tree in a container of water in an unheated place, such as a garage. Check the water level frequently. Trees can take in more than two quarts each day. If the tree is out of water for even a few hours, cut another half inch from the bottom of the trunk.

◆ *Small touches of evergreen lend a delightful note of holiday spirit to any room.*
Here, a tiny forest of terra-cotta-potted cedar, spruce, and pine are unadorned
except for gift-like arrangements of fruits and pine cones nestled at their base.

TABLETOP
TOPIARIES

*A*s fanciful in form and sweet in *fragrance as the larger trees they mimic, these topiaries will expand the frontiers of your Christmas forest.*

MATERIALS

Styrofoam block for base •
4" clay flower pot •
3 to 4 cinnamon sticks •
Florist wire or rubber band •
9" Styrofoam cone • *Evergreens* •
Clippers • *Glue gun* • *Sheet moss* •
Small pine cones (optional) •
Red berries (optional) •
Miniature ornaments (optional)

1. Wedge block of Styrofoam into clay pot.
2. Insert "tree trunk" of 3 to 4 cinnamon sticks. Bind tops together with florist wire or rubber band.
3. Hollow out base of Styrofoam cone with kitchen knife to accommodate cinnamon stick trunk.
4. Use gentle downward pressure to attach cone to trunk.
5. Beginning at base of cone and working toward the top, hot glue 3" sprigs of evergreens in layers, overlapping for dense coverage.
6. Cover Styrofoam base with sheet moss. Finish with small pine cones, red berries, or tiny ornaments, if you like.

WREATHS

STATICE WREATH

A *deep red bow provides a lively contrast to the soft glow of white statice.*

MATERIALS

Glue gun • *Fresh or dried German statice* •
10" grapevine wreath base • *Ribbon*

1. Use hot glue to secure short lengths of statice to wreath base.

2. Use generous length of ribbon to hang wreath, finishing with a bow.

PEPPER BERRY DOUBLE WREATH

A profusion of colorful pepper berries in a double wreath is accented with a lovely voile bow of soft moss green.

MATERIALS

14" grapevine wreath base •
10" grapevine wreath base •
Florist wire •
Monofilament •
Pepper berries • Ribbon •
14" lengths of grapevine •
Florist pick

1. Make small hanging loop with wire, then secure around 14" wreath base.
2. Working directly from the spool, tie monofilament end to wreath base.
3. Lay clusters of pepper berries on wreath, and use the traditional overhand wrapping method to secure pepper berries with monofilament. Tie off at end.
4. Repeat process on 10" wreath base.
5. Use monofilament or florist wire to join wreaths together.
6. Cover join with length of ribbon secured on back.
7. Bind 14" lengths of grapevine and attach to top of wreath with florist wire.
8. Wire bow onto florist pick; insert in wreath to finish.

MIXED GREENS WREATH

Evergreen, eucalyptus, pine cones, lady apples, pepper berries, dried citrus slices, and lavender combine to create a fragrant wreath.

MATERIALS

Florist wire • 18" by 22" oval grapevine wreath base • Cinnamon sticks • Dried lavender • Eucalyptus • Pepper berries • Pine cones • 4" florist picks • Lady apples • Dried citrus slices • Glue gun • Assorted evergreens, including cedar

1. Make small hanging loop with wire, then secure around wreath base.

2. Wire clusters of cinnamon sticks, lavender, eucalyptus, pepper berries, and pine cones to florist picks.

3. Insert picks into apple cores.

4. Hot glue dried citrus slices to florist picks.

5. Cover wreath base with evergreens and cedar, wedging stems securely into form.

6. Add all prepared elements on picks, securing with hot glue where necessary.

MOSS-LICHEN WREATH

*L*uminous white sola berries highlight the subtle earth *tones of dried florals.*

MATERIALS

Florist wire • 12" straw wreath base • Glue gun • Sheet moss • Lichen • Large and small pine cones • Dried white sola berries • 4" florist picks • Galax leaves

1. Make small hanging loop with wire, then secure around straw base.
2. Use hot glue to attach sheet moss and lichen.
3. Wire large pine cones and clusters of sola berries onto florist picks; insert into wreath.
4. Use hot glue to attach smaller pine cones and galax leaves.

GOLDEN ACORN WREATH

*G*race nooks and crannies with a few of these *simple wreaths.*

MATERIALS

16 gauge wire (approximately) • Needle nose pliers • Drill and 1/16" drill bit • Glue gun • Acorns • Gold spray paint • Evergreen sprigs • Florist wire • Ribbon

1. Cut wire to desired length; shape into an open circle.
2. Use pliers to create small hook at one end of wire.
3. Use drop of hot glue to secure acorn caps. Drill acorns and thread onto wire.
4. Join ends of wire circle and secure by crimping with pliers.
5. Working outside or in well-ventilated area, spray wreath with gold paint.
6. When completely dry, conceal join with evergreens, securing with florist wire.
7. Finish with ribbon.

BIRCH BARK
CORNUCOPIA

*B*ouquets of colorful red berries
and evergreens at every window
herald the joy of the season.

MATERIALS

*Birch bark cone • Small block of
Styrofoam • Birch twigs •
Evergreens • Seasonal berries*

1. Wedge block of Styrofoam
into birch bark cone.
2. Fill with birch twigs,
evergreens, and berries, inserting
stems securely in Styrofoam.

POMANDERS

The vibrant fragrance of clove-studded orange pomanders will fill the house with a subtle, spicy aroma. Make them by the score; add fancy cord or ribbon to some, so they can hang on the tree.

MATERIALS

Vegetable peeler or zester • Oranges • Cloves • Assorted greens

1. Use peeler to remove strips of orange peel in decorative patterns.

2. Insert cloves in grooves, allowing space for shrinkage.

3. Arrange in bowl with greens as desired.

ORANGE POMANDER ON DOORKNOB

The simplest details can delight and charm. As we pass from room to room, our pleasure is heightened by small surprises.

MATERIALS

Orange • Gold cording • Upholstery tacks (decorative furniture nails) • Assorted greens such as white pine, variegated ivy, and eucalyptus • Cinnamon sticks • Ribbon

1. Wrap orange with cording, as you would wrap a box, tying a knot, then making a loop for hanging.

2. Secure cording with upholstery tacks.

3. Hot glue sprigs of greens and cinnamon sticks.

4. Thread ribbon under cording and tie a bow.

FRUIT TOPIARIES

Create a miniature classical garden in a corner or on a tabletop.

MATERIALS

Styrofoam block for base • Container such as urn, pot, or vase • Styrofoam cone • 4" florist picks • Lemons, clementines, or strawberries • Boxwood

1. Wedge block of Styrofoam into container.

2. Secure cone in container with florist picks.

3. Starting at base of Styrofoam cone, use picks to secure fruit to cone.

4. Insert small sprigs of boxwood around each piece of fruit, filling in hollow spaces.

TIP: Use 4" picks for lemons and clementines; use toothpicks for strawberries, kumquats, cranberries, and other small fruits.

SUGARED FRUIT

Enchant your guests with this winter wonderland of fruits sparkling with sugar crystals. Accent with pine sprigs and bright red berries.

MATERIALS

Egg whites • 2 shallow bowls • Sugar crystals (from baking supply shops) • Pastry brush or soft bristled artist's brush • Assorted small fruit

1. Place egg whites in shallow bowl.
2. Put sugar crystals in another shallow bowl or plate.
3. Brush fruit with egg white, roll in sugar, and set aside to dry.
4. Arrange as desired.

CHRISTMAS STOCKINGS

*C*reate a mantelpiece heirloom or just a fun stocking.
Whether you use vintage fabric from the flea market,
scraps from a local fabric store, or old clothes ripe for recy-
cling, the stocking you make will be personal and unique.
Embellish them with colorful buttons, decorative fringes
and tassels, cords, ribbons, old embroidery and lace.

GREEN-STRIPED STOCKING

MATERIALS

½ yard striped fabric •
⅝ yard crochet trim, 5 inches wide

1. Enlarge pattern (see page 32). From fabric, cut
two stockings sections, one 18 x 2-inch cuff lining,
and one 6 ½ x 2-inch hanging loop.
2. All stitching is done in ½-inch seams, with right
sides facing, unless otherwise indicated. Pin and
stitch stocking sections, leaving upper edge open.
Clip curves and trim seams; turn right side out.
3. Fold trim in half crosswise; stitch one short side.
Stitch again close to first stitching; trim seam. Turn
right side out.
4. Fold lining in half crosswise; stitch short side.
Turn under ½ inch of one long edge; stitch close to
fold to hem.
5. Pin trim to upper edge of stocking, right sides up,
matching trim seam to back stocking seam. Pin
unhemmed edge of lining to upper edge of stocking,
on top of trim, with right sides facing; match lining
seam to trim seam. Stitch; trim seams. Flip lining
inside stocking.
6. Fold hanging loop in half lengthwise, with right
sides facing. Stitch long edge. Trim seam; turn right
side out. Fold loop in half crosswise, with raw ends
even; stitch loop inside upper back corner of stocking.

IVORY STOCKING

MATERIALS

½ yard ivory linen •
*18-inch-square embroidered
linen napkin*

1. Enlarge pattern (see page
32). From fabric, cut two
stocking sections, one 18 x 2-
inch cuff lining , and one 6 ½ x
2-inch hanging loop. From one
edge of napkin, cut 6 ½-inch
wide cuff.

2. All stitching is done in
½-inch seams, with right sides
facing, unless otherwise indicated. Pin and stitch stocking
sections, leaving upper edge
open. Clip curves and trim
seams; turn right side out.

3. Fold lining in half crosswise;
stitch short side. Turn under
½ inch of one long edge; stitch
close to fold to hem.

4. Pin raw edge of cuff to
upper edge of stocking, right
sides up, matching cuff seam to
back stocking seam. Pin
unhemmed edge of lining to
upper edge of stocking, on top
of trim, with right sides facing;
match lining seam to cuff seam.
Stitch; trim seams. Flip lining
inside stocking.

5. Fold hanging loop in half
lengthwise, with right sides
facing. Stitch long edge. Trim
seam; turn right side out. Fold
loop in half crosswise, with raw
ends even; stitch loop inside
upper back corner of stocking.

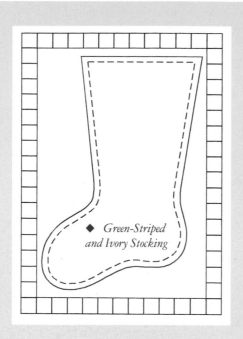

◆ *Green-Striped and Ivory Stocking*

◆ *Each square equals 1 inch. Connect lines across pattern pieces to form a grid. Or enlarge to 615 percent using a photocopier.*

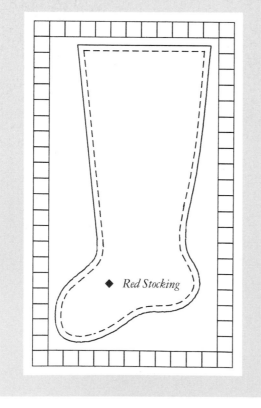

◆ *Red Stocking*

RED STOCKING

MATERIALS

¾ yard lightweight tapestry fabric ●
⅝ yard fringe trim, 1 ¾ inches wide

1. Enlarge pattern (see below left). From fabric, cut two stocking sections, one 20 x 2-inch cuff lining, and one 6 ½ x 2-inch hanging loop.

2. All stitching is done in ½-inch seams, with right sides facing, unless otherwise indicated. Pin and stitch stocking sections, leaving upper edge open. Clip curves and trim seams; turn right side out.

3. Fold lining in half crosswise; stitch short side. Turn under ½ inch of one long edge; stitch close to fold to hem.

4. Pin raw edge of lining to upper edge of stocking, matching lining seam to back stocking seam. Stitch; trim seams. Flip lining inside stocking.

5. Pin trim to upper edge of stocking, with right side up, and stitch, overlapping trim ends at back stocking seam.

6. Fold hanging loop in half lengthwise, with right sides facing. Stitch long edge. Trim seam; turn right side out. Fold loop in half crosswise, with raw ends even; stitch loop inside upper back corner of stocking.

BLUE-STRIPED STOCKING

MATERIALS

⅜ yard blue striped fabric ●
¼ yard muslin ●
⅝ yard embroidered trim, 1 inch wide

1. Enlarge pattern (see opposite page). From striped fabric, cut two stocking sections and one 14 x 5-inch cuff (cut on bias). From muslin, cut one 14 x 5-inch cuff lining and one 6 ½ x 2-inch hanging loop.

2. All stitching is done in ½-inch seams, with right sides facing, unless otherwise indicated. Pin and stitch stocking sections, leaving upper edge open. Clip curves and trim seams; turn right side out.

3. Fold cuff in half crosswise; stitch short side. Trim seam. Turn right side out.

4. Cut 14 inches of trim. Fold in half crosswise; stitch short end. Pin trim to one edge of cuff, with upper edge of trim even with raw edge of cuff and seams aligned.

5. Fold lining in half crosswise; stitch short side. Trim seam. Pin lining over cuff, right sides facing, with upper edge of lining even with trimmed edge of cuff and seams aligned. Stitch ¼ inch from trimmed edge of cuff; turn right side out. Baste raw edges of lined cuff together.

6. Place lined cuff inside stocking, with right sides out. Pin cuff to upper edge of stocking, raw edges even and seams aligned at stocking back. Stitch raw edges together; trim seam. Fold cuff to outside of stocking.

7. Fold hanging loop in half lengthwise, with right sides facing. Stitch long edge. Trim seam; turn right side out. Cut 6½ inches of trim. Turn under long edges of trim so embroidery is centered and trim is ½ inch wide. Pin trim to loop, right sides out; stitch along long edges of trim. Fold loop in half crosswise, with raw ends even and trimmed side out; stitch loop inside upper back corner of stocking.

TOILE STOCKING

MATERIALS

⅝ yard toile fabric •
Frog closure

1. Enlarge pattern (see right). From fabric, cut two stocking sections, two 18 x 5-inch cuff sections, one 18 x 2-inch cuff lining, and one 6 ½ x 2-inch hanging loop.

2. All stitching is done in ½-inch seams, with right sides facing, unless otherwise indicated. Pin and stitch stocking sections, leaving upper edge open. Clip curves and trim seams; turn right side out.

3. Pin and stitch cuff sections together along one long and two short edges. Trim corners; turn right side out. Baste raw edges together.

4. Fold lining in half crosswise; stitch short end. Turn under ½ inch of one long edge; stitch close to fold to hem.

5. Pin raw edge of cuff to upper edge of stocking, with right sides out, so short ends of cuff meet at center of one side of stocking. Pin unhemmed edge of lining to upper edge of stocking, over cuff, with right sides facing; match lining seam to back stocking seam. Stitch long edge; trim seams. Flip lining inside stocking.

6. Center frog closure over open ends of cuff on stocking side. Hand-stitch frog to cuff.

7. Fold hanging loop in half lengthwise, with right sides facing. Stitch long edge. Trim seam; turn right side out. Fold loop in half crosswise, with raw ends even; stitch loop inside upper back corner of stocking.

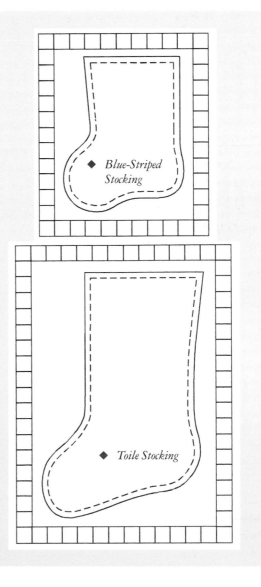

◆ *Blue-Striped Stocking*

◆ *Toile Stocking*

LITTLE ANGELS
PAJAMAS

*H*and-painted or stenciled, basic pajamas become cheerful *works of art. For a special photo-op, make matching parent-child T-shirts.*

To decorate crawlers, T-shirts, sweatshirts, long johns, or other cotton garment (see Sources, page 156), you will need paint pens, fabric paints, and stencils.

To make freehand designs, use paint pens sold in crafts stores: Just squeeze to release paint, then draw snowflakes or trees. You can also draw your design first with washable fabric marker, then go over it with paint. Let dry 4 to 6 hours.

To make stenciled garments, use store-bought stencils and fabric paints. Stencil a sample on paper first, then lay garment flat and stencil with a stencil brush, one side at a time. (Use very little paint on brush; lift and move stencil carefully to avoid smudges.) Let first side dry 1 hour, then turn garment over; stencil second side and let dry at least 1 hour.

DÉCOUPAGE
PLATE

A glass plate becomes a unique heirloom with fruit botanicals set against a palette of old-style script for an antique effect.

MATERIALS

Gift wrap, old cards, family photos, or other documents • Plaid Treasure Gold • Clear glass plate (see Sources, page 156) • Scissors • 1" foam brush • Plaid Royal Coat découpage finish • Acrylic craft paint

1. Make color photocopies of photos and other items you don't wish to cut up. Enlarge or reduce images as desired.
2. Apply Treasure Gold to reverse edge of plate using fingertip or small brush. Allow to dry.
3. Carefully trim items and arrange composition.
4. Brush a light coat of Royal Coat on back of plate, place first item on surface, then use fingers to smooth in place. Smooth out bubbles and edges.
5. Repeat for all cutouts. They should be smooth and completely dry before continuing.
6. Using foam brush, cover entire surface with Royal Coat. When dry and clear, approximately 10 to 20 minutes, repeat.
7. When completely dry, apply two coats of craft paint to plate back.

DECORATING *the* TREE

Custom and ritual surround the finished tree, as each year we retrieve our treasured ornaments from dark and dust, then wrap them one by one at season's end in anticipation of Christmases to come.

This tree, bejeweled with old-fashioned glass globes and adorned with homespun felt cones filled with dried flowers and giant golden paper stars, is an enchanting combination.

ORNAMENTS

Handcrafted ornaments will give your tree a truly personal touch. As this host of ornaments shows, simple forms and natural objects are easily dressed up with gold cord, ribbon, and spray paint.

RED GLASS ORNAMENT

MATERIALS

Gold grosgrain ribbon • Glass ornament • Glue gun • Red and gold cording • Scissors

1. Cut 2 strips of gold ribbon to wrap around glass ball; glue in place.
2. Wrap cording over ribbon and around ornament's wire hanging loop; secure with a few dots of hot glue.
3. Thread another strip of gold ribbon through wire hanging loop.

LEMON AND RIBBON ORNAMENT

MATERIALS

Velvet and satin ribbons • Dried lemon • Glue gun • Upholstery tacks (decorative furniture nails) • Scissors

1. Make overhand knot in ribbon for hanging loop.
2. Secure loop to top of lemon with dot of hot glue; continue wrapping ribbon around lemon. Cut ribbon at loop and secure with glue.
3. Cut second strip of ribbon and glue around circumference of lemon.
4. Anchor ribbon at intersections with upholstery tacks.

GILDED ACORNS

MATERIALS

Acorns or purchased wooden acorns • Glue gun • Plaid Mod Podge • Paint brush • Imitation gold-leaf (Dutch Metal) • Gold string

1. If using natural acorns, secure caps to nut with hot glue.
2. Apply thin coat of Mod Podge to acorn with paint brush.
3. Apply small squares of imitation gold leaf to acorn, gently pressing edges down.
4. When dry, wind gold string around acorn stem and secure with drop of hot glue.

GOLDEN NUT CLUSTERS

MATERIALS

Assorted nuts • Gold spray paint •
Glue gun • Gold crinkle wire •
Gold ribbon

1. Spray nuts with gold paint; allow
to dry.
2. Dab drops of hot glue on nuts to
create a cluster.
3. Randomly wrap glued cluster with
crinkle wire.
4. Use gold ribbon for hanging loop and
bow; secure with hot glue.

FROSTED ARTICHOKE ORNAMENT

MATERIALS

Plaid Treasure Gold •
Dried artichoke • Paint brush •
Glue gun • Ribbon •
Plaid Mod Podge • Artificial
snow • Clear glitter

1. Following manufacturer's
instructions, gild dried artichoke
with Treasure Gold using finger
or brush.
2. Hot glue a hanging loop of
ribbon on artichoke stem.
3. Brush Mod Podge on leaves
nearest stem; add artificial snow
and glitter.

SHINY LEMON ORNAMENT

MATERIALS

Gold ribbon • Dried lemon •
Glue gun • Upholstery tacks
(decorative furniture nails) •
Gold crinkle wire •
Silver crinkle wire

1. Cut short length of ribbon for
hanging loop.
2. Attach loop to end of lemon
with hot glue.
3. Insert tacks at both ends
of lemon.
4. Wrap lemon with gold and
silver crinkle wire, anchoring
at tacks.

KISSING BALLS

A lso known as kissing boughs or bunches, kissing balls evoke the time when they whimsically graced Victorian parlors. Kissing balls can be made in an array of styles and color schemes to complement any seasonal decor. Here, evergreen sprigs, miniature pine cones, and red berries are attached to florist picks with florist's wire and inserted into a 10-inch Styrofoam ball, then embellished with a plaid bow at top and bottom. The final touch is a loop for hanging.

GILDED KISSING BALL

MATERIALS

Florist wire or kitchen twine for hanging •
4" Styrofoam ball • Assorted nuts •
Gold spray paint • 4" florist picks • Glue gun •
Evergreens such as balsam • Gold organza ribbon

1. Make hanging loop of wire or twine; wrap around ball to secure.

2. Spray nuts with gold paint; allow to dry.

3. Attach nuts to 4" florist picks with drop of hot glue.

4. Insert evergreen sprigs into ball to desired lengths.

5. Insert nuts.

6. Add ribbon, securing with short loops of wire pushed into ball.

LUMINARIA

Twinkling lights against the early darkness of winter are a cheery and simple pleasure of the holiday season. An enchanting display need not be elaborate or difficult to produce. With a bit of imagination, everyday items can be used to charming effect. This sparkling version of the traditional paper-bag luminaria is created using a five-gallon bucket from the hardware store.

Fill with snow or white sand to within four inches of the bucket's rim; place a pillar candle in the center and firmly pack additional snow or sand around the candle. Embellish with seasonal berries or greens. Even flea-market finds like old-fashioned lanterns can provide inspiration. Hang them with sturdy ribbon on the bare branches of a tree or from the beams of a porch for an appealing display.

CHRISTMAS
GLOW

Lighting plays a central role in creating the right ambiance for any festive gathering and there's nothing more appealing than the soft glow of candles. Easy-to-make candle centerpieces can be wonderfully creative: The natural rustic simplicity of cinnamon sticks bound with raffia in this centerpiece almost suggests a pioneer settlement built in the wilderness. A garland-wrapped lamppost, here with the electric bulb replaced by a candle, imparts a romantic and nostalgic mood.

CENTERPIECES

FLORAL AND CANDLE CENTERPIECE

The bright purple-pink and red of the anemones in this grouping are deftly highlighted by the light green of the limes and the warm brown tones of the cinnamon sticks.

MATERIALS

Block of oasis • Pillar candles • Cinnamon sticks • Oval platter • Fresh flowers and greens such as anemones, ranuncula, eucalyptus, and cedar • Pine cones • Limes

1. Submerge oasis in water until saturated. Allow to drain, then cut into 3" squares.
2. Arrange candles and cinnamon sticks on platter.
3. Place blocks of oasis between candles, and fill with flowers and greens.
4. Finish with pine cones and limes.

CRANBERRY FLORAL CENTERPIECE

*U*se cranberries instead of florists' marbles to hold stems in a crystal vase and experiment with different combinations of fresh flowers and greenery.

MATERIALS

Glass cylinder vase • Fresh or frozen whole cranberries • Assorted fresh flowers such as roses, hyacinths, tulips, and paperwhites

1. Partially fill container with water; add cranberries.
2. Arrange flowers, hiding stems in berries. Depending on amount of displacement, you may need to add or remove some berries.

HURRICANE LAMP FLORAL CENTERPIECE

A quaint hurricane lamp, rising up as if from an island paradise, anchors this arrangement to your table. The trailing ivy provides movement and visual flow.

MATERIALS

12" oasis ring •
Assorted greens, flowers and herbs such as eucalyptus, ivy, rosemary, anemones, and ranunculas

1. Submerge oasis ring in water until saturated. Allow to drain.
2. Cut and insert greens.
3. Cut and insert flowers.
4. Place around base of hurricane lantern.

RIBBON AND CARD GARLAND

Display the beautiful images and messages from friends and loved ones on pretty ribbon entwined in a fresh green garland. And let paper snowflakes dance on your windowpanes.

MATERIALS

White bond paper • Sharp scissors • Dry iron • Spray adhesive • Wired ribbon • Fresh garland

1. Fold paper in half lengthwise, then widthwise.

2. Make 45-degree fold to make a triangle. Cut away excess strip at top.

3. Create design by cutting strips and triangles from three sides. Check your progress periodically.

4. Press with a warm iron to flatten. Lightly coat with spray adhesive to prevent curling on glass panes. Press into place. (Spray adhesive will come off with window cleaner.)

5. Wrap ribbon around garland. Tack to corners, framing window.

6. Add corner bows and ribbon streamers onto which to tape cards.

◆ *Coordinate your holiday decor and tree by using the same colors and motifs for both.*

WINDOW SWAGS

Bring in the outdoors to dress your windows! You can collect seasonal greens from your own yard and simply wire them into "L" shapes. And with no more than well-placed bows at the corners, you'll create beautiful, traditional holiday swags. To complete the wintry scene, sprigs of green brightly embellish the windowpanes.

GIFT-WRAPPED PILLOWS

Tie wide ribbon bows around occasional pillows as you would on presents and scatter on couches and chairs.

BUTTON WREATH

Miniature wreaths like this one of colorful buttons add a playful note to any doorknob or cabinet. Choose strong thin wire that will hold a circular shape and include a diverse array of button colors and sizes.

GILDED PEAR PLACE MARKER

Beckon your guests to the table by name with beguiling golden-pear place markers.

MATERIALS

Plaid Treasure Gold • Pear with stem •
Small blank card • Gold marker •
Hole punch • Ribbon

1. Use finger to apply Treasure Gold to pear.
Allow to dry.

2. Write guest's name on card with gold marker.
Punch hole in one corner.

3. Attach card to pear stem with ribbon.

Entertaining

*S*haring the joy of the season with festive foods and sweet indulgences is as much a part of the celebration as the Christmas tree. Pick and choose among these best-ever holiday recipes to present a Yuletide feast or to entertain friends at a casual get-together. And so no one is left out, we've included a children's party theme. Here are a few tips.

• To avoid an exhausting last minute rush of trying to get too many things done in too little time, set a schedule for completing as many tasks as possible in advance of the event.

• Start your holiday baking right after Thanksgiving. Many cookie doughs can be frozen for up to two months. Depending upon type, finished baked goods, when properly wrapped, can be frozen one to three months.

• Complete as much of the food preparation ahead as possible. Many of the appetizers and side dishes in the following pages include do-ahead instructions.

• Be prepared for unexpected guests by stocking the pantry with savories for short-cut appetizers. Marinated artichokes, tapenade, fancy nuts, pâté, assorted cheeses, and crackers are great hurry-up hors d'oeuvres.
• Remember, this is the season of good cheer and fellowship. Relax and have fun!

• Lists are the easiest way to get organized. Have a master "To Do" list plus individual lists for specific tasks. When entertaining always have a guest list, a menu list, and two shopping lists for nonperishable and perishable items.

• Early in December: Purchase nonperishable foodstuffs. Stock bar supplies, including soft drinks. Count chairs, glasses, serving dishes, and utensils; borrow, buy, or rent what you need.

Appetizers

POTATO NESTS

PREP: 45 MINUTES PLUS CHILLING
BAKE: 31 TO 33 MINUTES

2 large baking potatoes (1 ½ pounds), unpeeled
½ cup sour cream
1 tablespoon prepared white horseradish
1 tablespoon chopped fresh dill
½ teaspoon salt
⅛ teaspoon ground black pepper
dill sprigs and/or smoked salmon for topping
  (optional)
pepper slices and radish for garnish

1. In 3-quart saucepan, combine potatoes and enough *water* to cover; heat to boiling over high heat. Reduce heat; cover and simmer 20 minutes, or until potatoes are just cooked through. Drain potatoes; refrigerate about 1 hour or until chilled.

2. Meanwhile, in small bowl, mix sour cream, horseradish, and dill until blended. Cover and refrigerate until ready to serve.

3. Preheat oven to 425°F. Grease thirty-two 1¾" by 1" mini muffin-pan cups.

4. Peel and coarsely grate potatoes. In medium bowl, gently toss grated potatoes with salt and pepper. Place about 1 heaping measuring tablespoon potato mixture in each mini muffin-pan cup; press mixture against bottom and up sides of cups, allowing some mixture to extend slightly above rim.

5. Bake potato nests 25 minutes, or until edges are golden brown. Cover pans loosely with foil if nests brown too quickly. Cool nests in pans on wire rack 10 minutes. Carefully transfer potato nests to jelly-roll pan or cookie sheet lined with paper towels. Let stand at room temperature up to 4 hours before serving.

6. To serve, preheat oven to 375°F. Place nests on large cookie sheet (without paper towels), and bake 6 to 8 minutes, until heated through and crisp. Transfer nests to platter. Spoon about 1 teaspoon sour-cream mixture into each nest, and top each with a dill sprig or a small piece of smoked salmon, if you like. Garnish plate with pepper slices and radish. Makes 32 nests.

Each filled nest without topping: About 20 calories, 0 g protein, 3 g carbohydrate, 1 g total fat (1 g saturated), 2 mg cholesterol, 40 mg sodium.

◆ *Potato Nests*

◆ *Appetizers are versatile tidbits that can be appetite teasers for the courses to follow or the makings of a whole meal. Allow 4 to 5 per guest when a meal is to follow, 10 to 12 when no other food will be served. So that guests can easily and neatly manage to hold and eat them, keep appetizers bite-size.*

◆ *Olive Twists*

OLIVE TWISTS

PREP: 30 MINUTES
BAKE: 12 TO 15 MINUTES PER BATCH

1 package (8 ounces) feta cheese, well drained
  and crumbled
⅓ cup chopped fresh parsley
⅓ cup olive paste or ½ cup Kalamata olives,
  pitted and pureed with 1 tablespoon olive oil
2 large egg whites
1 package (17¼ ounces) frozen puff-pastry
  sheets, thawed

1. Preheat oven to 400°F. In small bowl, with fork, mix feta cheese, parsley, olive paste, and egg whites until thoroughly blended; set aside.

2. On lightly floured surface, unfold 1 pastry sheet, keeping other sheet refrigerated. Using floured rolling pin, roll out pastry sheet into 16" by 14" rectangle.

Cut pastry in half crosswise. Spread half of olive mixture evenly over 1 pastry half; top with remaining pastry half. Using rolling pin, gently roll over pastry layers to seal them together.

3. Grease large cookie sheet. With large chef's knife, cut pastry rectangle crosswise into ½-inch-wide strips, taking care not to tear pastry. Twist each strip 3 to 4 times, then place strips about 1 inch apart on cookie sheet.

4. Bake strips 12 to 15 minutes, until pastry is puffed and lightly browned. With wide spatula, transfer sticks to wire rack to cool. Repeat with remaining pastry sheet and olive mixture. Serve at room temperature. Store in tightly covered container. Makes about 56 twists.

Each twist: About 55 calories, 1 g protein, 5 g carbohydrate, 4 g total fat (1 g saturated), 4 mg cholesterol, 80 mg sodium.

PICKLED VEGETABLES

PREP: 30 MINUTES PLUS OVERNIGHT TO CHILL

*2 bags (16 ounces each) carrots, peeled and cut into
    4" by ¼" matchstick strips*
1 pound green beans, trimmed
*1 medium head cauliflower (2 pounds), separated
    into flowerets*
*1 small bunch celery, cut into 4" by ½"
    matchstick strips*
3 cups cider vinegar
⅓ cup sugar
2 teaspoons salt
1 cup water
1 can (7 ¼ ounces drained) large ripe olives
2 bunches radishes

1. Blanch vegetables (except celery): In 4-quart
saucepan, heat *2 inches water* to boiling over high heat.
Add carrots; heat to boiling. Cook 1 to 2 minutes,
until tender-crisp. With slotted spoon, transfer carrots
to bowl of cold water to stop cooking; drain well.
Repeat with green beans and cauliflower.
2. Prepare marinade: In 1-cup glass measuring
cup, mix ¾ cup vinegar, 4 teaspoons sugar, ½ teaspoon salt, and ¼ cup water. Pour marinade into large
zip-tight plastic bag. (Repeat for each vegetable, fol
lowing instructions below for flavoring.)
3. Place each vegetable in its marinade. Close bag and
refrigerate up to 2 days, turning occasionally.
4. To serve, drain marinade from each vegetable.
Arrange all pickled vegetables on tray or platter with
olives and radishes. Makes 12 first-course servings.

Each serving: About 90 calories, 3 g protein, 16 g carbohydrate, 4 g total fat (0 g saturated), 0 mg cholesterol, 240 mg sodium.

LEMON-TARRAGON CELERY: Prepare basic marinade as in step 2, but add 1 teaspoon dried tarragon
and strips of peel from 1 lemon. Marinate and serve as
in steps 3 and 4.

PEPPERCORN-DILL CARROTS: Blanch and cool
carrots as in step 1. Prepare basic marinade as in step
2, but add ¼ cup chopped fresh dill (or 2 teaspoons
dried dillweed) and 1 teaspoon whole black peppercorns. Marinate and serve as in steps 3 and 4.

SPICED CAULIFLOWER: Blanch and cool cauliflower as in step 1. Prepare basic marinade as in step 2,
but add 1 tablespoon pickling spice. Marinate and
serve as in step 3 and 4.

ORANGE-FENNEL GREEN BEANS: Blanch and
cool beans as in step 1. Prepare basic marinade as in
step 2, but add 1 teaspoon fennel seeds, crushed, and
strips of peel from 1 small orange. Marinate and serve
as in steps 3 and 4.

CAVIAR PIE

PREP: 25 MINUTES
COOK: 15 MINUTES PLUS STANDING

8 large eggs
⅓ cup mayonnaise
¼ cup chopped fresh dill or parsley
¼ teaspoon salt
¼ teaspoon ground black pepper
1 container (8 ounces) sour cream
1 jar (2 ounces) red lumpfish caviar

1. In 3-quart saucepan, combine eggs and enough *cold
water* to cover eggs by at least 1 inch; heat to boiling
over high heat. Remove saucepan from heat and cover;
let stand 15 minutes. Pour off hot water and run cold
water over eggs to cool. Remove shells.
2. In bowl, with pastry blender or fork, mash eggs.
Stir in mayonnaise, dill, salt, pepper, and 2 tablespoons
sour cream. Spoon mixture into 9-inch pie plate.
Cover and refrigerate overnight or until ready to serve.
3. To serve, spread remaining sour cream evenly over
egg mixture; top with caviar. Makes about 3 cups.

Each tablespoon: About 35 calories, 2 g protein, 0 g
carbohydrate, 3 g total fat (1 g saturated), 45 mg cholesterol, 50 mg sodium.

MEXICAN SHRIMP SKEWERS

PREP: 45 MINUTES
COOK: 3 MINUTES

40 *large shrimp (1 ¾ pounds), shelled and deveined*
1 *can (4 to 4 ½ ounces) mild green chiles, chopped, with their juice*
2 *tablespoons fresh lime juice*
1 *tablespoon chopped fresh cilantro or 1 teaspoon dried cilantro*
1 *tablespoon olive or vegetable oil*
½ *teaspoon sugar*
¾ *teaspoon salt*
½ *teaspoon ground black pepper*
2 *medium avocados*
20 *(12-inch) bamboo skewers*
lime and lemon wedges for garnish

1. In 4-quart saucepan, heat *8 cups water* to boiling over high heat. Add shrimp and heat to boiling; cook 1 to 2 minutes, until shrimp turn opaque. Drain.
2. In large bowl, combine chiles, lime juice, cilantro, oil, sugar, salt, and pepper. Add shrimp and stir to coat thoroughly with dressing. If not serving kabobs right away, cover and refrigerate shrimp mixture.
3. Just before serving, cut each avocado in half lengthwise. With sharp knife, remove pit. Peel and cut avocados into 1 ¼-inch chunks. Gently stir avocado into shrimp mixture until thoroughly coated with chile dressing, being careful not to bruise avocado.
4. On each skewer, thread 2 shrimp and 2 chunks of avocado. Arrange skewers on large platter; garnish with lime and lemon wedges. Serve immediately. Makes 20 appetizers.

Each appetizer: About 49 calories, 3 g protein, 1 g carbohydrate, 4 g total fat (1 g saturated), 22 mg cholesterol, 127 mg sodium.

◆ *Mexican Shrimp Skewers*

◆ *Christmas Quesadillas*

CHRISTMAS QUESADILLAS

PREP: 40 MINUTES
BAKE: 8 MINUTES

1 tablespoon vegetable oil
1 large onion, finely chopped
1 green pepper, finely chopped
1 red pepper, finely chopped
1 garlic clove, finely chopped
¼ teaspoon ground cumin
¼ teaspoon salt
2 tablespoons chopped fresh cilantro
12 (6- to 7-inch) flour tortillas
6 ounces Monterey Jack cheese with jalapeño chiles,
 shredded (1½ cups)
cilantro leaves and 1 hot red pepper for garnish

1. In nonstick 10-inch skillet, heat oil over medium heat. Add onion and peppers; cook, stirring often,

15 minutes, or until golden and tender. Add garlic, cumin, and salt and cook, stirring often, 5 minutes longer. Remove skillet from heat; stir in cilantro.

2. Place 6 tortillas on work surface. Spread pepper mixture on tortillas; sprinkle with cheese. Top with remaining tortillas to make 6 quesadillas. If not serving right away, cover and refrigerate assembled quesadillas up to 6 hours.

3. To serve, preheat oven to 450°F. Place quesadillas on 2 large cookie sheets and bake 4 minutes per side, or until lightly browned. Transfer quesadillas to cutting board. Cut each into 8 wedges; top each wedge with a cilantro leaf for garnish. Garnish platter with a hot red pepper. Serve immediately. Makes 48 wedges.

Each wedge: About 50 calories, 2 g protein, 6 g carbohydrate, 2 g total fat (1 g saturated), 4 mg cholesterol, 75 mg sodium.

PIMIENTO-STUDDED DEVILED EGGS

PREP: 40 MINUTES

> 12 large eggs, hard-cooked and shelled
> ¼ cup sliced pimientos, chopped
> ¼ cup low-fat mayonnaise dressing
> 1 tablespoon plus 1 teaspoon Dijon mustard
> ½ teaspoon ground red pepper (cayenne)
> ¼ teaspoon salt
> fresh herb sprigs for garnish

1. Slice each egg lengthwise in half. Gently remove yolks and place in small bowl; with fork, thoroughly mash yolks. Add pimientos, mayonnaise dressing, mustard, ground red pepper, and salt and stir until well mixed.

2. Place egg-white halves in 15½" by 10½" jelly-roll pan lined with paper towels (to prevent eggs from rolling). Spoon yolk mixture into egg-white halves. Cover and refrigerate until ready to serve. Makes 24 appetizers.

Each appetizer: About 45 calories, 3 g protein, 1 g carbohydrate, 3 g total fat (1 g saturated), 107 mg cholesterol, 100 mg sodium.

SMOKED TROUT PÂTÉ

PREP: 30 MINUTES

> 3 whole smoked trout (1 ¼ pounds)
> 1 package (8 ounces) whipped cream cheese
> ¼ cup low-fat mayonnaise dressing
> 3 tablespoons lemon juice
> ⅛ teaspoon ground black pepper
> 1 tablespoon finely chopped chives or green onion chives for garnish
> assorted crackers and cucumber slices

1. Cut head and tail from each trout; remove skin and bones and discard. In food processor with knife blade attached, puree trout, cream cheese, mayonnaise dressing, lemon juice, and black pepper until smooth.

2. Spoon trout mixture into medium bowl; stir in finely chopped chives. Cover and refrigerate if not serving right away.

3. To serve, allow refrigerated pâté to stand at room temperature 15 minutes to soften. Garnish with chives. Serve with crackers and cucumber slices. Makes about 3 cups.

Each tablespoon pâté without crackers or cucumbers: About 35 calories, 2 g protein, 1 g carbohydrate, 3 g total fat (1 g saturated), 7 mg cholesterol, 100 mg sodium.

SESAME PITA TOASTS

PREP: 25 MINUTES
BAKE: 8 MINUTES

> ½ cup sesame seeds, toasted
> 2 tablespoons chopped fresh parsley
> 2 teaspoons dried thyme
> 2 teaspoons grated lemon peel
> ½ teaspoon salt
> ¼ teaspoon coarsely ground black pepper
> 1 package (7 ounces) 2-inch mini pitas
> 2 tablespoons extra virgin olive oil

1. Prepare spice mixture: In blender, blend sesame seeds, parsley, thyme, lemon peel, salt, and pepper, stopping blender occasionally and scraping down sides with rubber spatula, until seeds are ground. Transfer spice mixture to medium bowl.

2. Brush tops of pitas with oil. Sprinkle oiled side of each pita with about 1½ teaspoons spice mixture; gently press spices onto pita. Place pitas on large cookie sheet. If not serving right away, cover and refrigerate up to 6 hours.

3. To serve, preheat oven to 450°F. Bake 8 minutes, or until pitas are crisp and golden. Makes 24 toasts.

Each toast: About 50 calories, 1 g protein, 5 g carbohydrate, 3 g total fat (0 g saturated), 0 mg cholesterol, 75 mg sodium.

◆ *Pimiento-Studded Deviled Eggs and Smoked Trout Pâté*

◆ *Lacy Parmesan Crisps*

LACY PARMESAN CRISPS

PREP: 20 MINUTES

BAKE: 6 TO 7 MINUTES PER BATCH

6 ounces Parmesan cheese, coarsely shredded
(1 ½ cups)

1. Preheat oven to 375°F. Line large cookie sheet with reusable nonstick bakeware liner (see Sources, page 156). Spoon cheese by level measuring tablespoons, about 3 inches apart, onto cookie sheet. Spread each spoonful into 2-inch round.

2. Bake cheese rounds 6 to 7 minutes, until edges just begin to color. Transfer bakeware liner to wire rack; cool 2 minutes. Transfer crisps to paper towels. Repeat with remaining cheese. Store in airtight container up to 4 days. Makes about 2 dozen crisps.

Each crisp: About 30 calories, 3 g protein, 0 g carbohydrate, 2 g total fat (1 g saturated), 6 mg cholesterol, 130 mg sodium.

ROASTED RED PEPPER AND WALNUT DIP

PREP: 30 MINUTES PLUS COOLING
BROIL: 10 MINUTES

4 medium red peppers
½ cup walnuts
½ teaspoon ground cumin
2 slices firm white bread, torn into pieces
2 tablespoons raspberry vinegar
1 tablespoon olive oil
½ teaspoon salt
⅛ teaspoon ground red pepper (cayenne)
toasted pita triangles

1. Preheat broiler; line broiling pan with foil. Broil peppers at closest position to heat source, turning occasionally, 10 minutes, or until charred and blistered all over. Remove from broiler. Wrap peppers loosely in foil and allow to steam at room temperature 15 minutes, or until cool enough to handle.
2. Turn oven control to 350°F. Spread walnuts in 9" by 9" metal baking pan and bake 8 to 10 minutes, until toasted. In 1-quart saucepan, toast cumin over low heat 1 to 2 minutes, until very fragrant.
3. Remove peppers from foil; peel off skin; discard skin and seeds. Cut peppers into large pieces. In food processor with knife blade attached, process walnuts until ground. Add roasted peppers, cumin, bread, raspberry vinegar, oil, salt, and ground red pepper; puree until smooth. Transfer to bowl. Cover and refrigerate if not serving right away. Remove from refrigerator 30 minutes before serving. Serve with toasted pita triangles. Makes about 2 cups dip.

Each tablespoon: About 25 calories, 0 g protein, 2 g carbohydrate, 2 g total fat (0 g saturated), 0 mg cholesterol, 40 mg sodium.

OMELET ESPAÑOLA SQUARES

PREP: 45 MINUTES
BAKE: 15 TO 20 MINUTES

2 tablespoons olive oil
2 large all-purpose potatoes (1 pound), chopped
1 medium onion, sliced
1 medium green pepper, finely chopped
¾ teaspoon salt
8 large eggs
¼ teaspoon coarsely ground black pepper
½ cup water
1 can (14½ ounces) diced tomatoes, drained
½ cup chopped pimiento-stuffed olives (salad olives)
fresh chives for garnish (optional)

1. In nonstick 10-inch skillet with oven-safe handle (or wrap handle with heavy-duty foil for baking in oven later), heat oil over medium heat. Add potatoes, onion, green pepper, and ¼ teaspoon salt and cook, stirring occasionally, about 20 minutes, until vegetables are tender.
2. Meanwhile, preheat oven to 400°F. In medium bowl, with wire whisk or fork, beat eggs with pepper remaining ½ teaspoon salt, and water. Stir in tomatoes and olives. Stir egg mixture into potato mixture in skillet; cover and cook 5 minutes, or until egg mixture begins to set around edge. Remove cover and place skillet in oven; bake 15 to 20 minutes, until omelet is set.
3. Carefully invert omelet onto large flat plate. Let cool before cutting into 1-inch squares. Garnish with chives. Makes about 60 squares.

Each square: About 25 calories, 1 g protein, 2 g carbohydrate, 1 g total fat (0 g saturated), 28 mg cholesterol, 100 mg sodium.

Soups

CAULIFLOWER-CHEDDAR SOUP

PREP: 35 MINUTES
COOK: 25 MINUTES

2 tablespoons butter or margarine
1 medium onion, chopped
¼ cup all-purpose flour
½ teaspoon salt
2 cups milk
1 can (14½ ounces) chicken broth
1½ cups water
1 head cauliflower (2½ pounds), cut into
    1-inch pieces
1 teaspoon Dijon mustard
1 package (8 ounces) shredded sharp Cheddar
    cheese (2 cups)

1. In 4-quart saucepan, melt butter over medium heat. Add onion and cook, stirring occasionally, about 10 minutes, until golden. Stir in flour and salt; cook, stirring frequently, 2 minutes. Gradually stir in milk, broth, and water. Add cauliflower and heat to boiling over high heat. Reduce heat; cover and simmer about 10 minutes, until cauliflower is tender.

2. In blender, with center part of blender cover removed to allow steam to escape, puree cauliflower mixture in small batches until smooth. Pour pureed mixture into large bowl after each batch.

3. Return mixture to saucepan; heat soup, stirring occasionally, until hot. Remove saucepan from heat; stir in mustard and 1½ cups cheese until melted and smooth. Garnish soup with remaining cheese to serve. Makes about 9 cups or 8 first-course servings.

Each serving: About 230 calories, 14 g carbohydrates, 13 g protein, 15 g total fat (8 g saturated), 41 mg cholesterol, 575 mg sodium.

GREEN GUMBO

PREP: 20 MINUTES
COOK: 40 MINUTES

8 slices bacon, cut into ½-inch pieces
¼ cup all-purpose flour
1 teaspoon salt
¼ teaspoon ground red pepper (cayenne)
2 cans (14½ ounces each) chicken broth
1½ pounds fresh greens (collard or mustard, or a
    combination), coarse stems removed and leaves
    cut into ½-inch pieces
1 package (10 ounces) frozen chopped spinach,
    thawed and squeezed dry
1 large all-purpose potato (8 ounces), peeled
    and grated
4 cups water

1. In 5-quart Dutch oven, cook bacon over medium-low heat until browned. With slotted spoon, transfer bacon to paper towels to drain. Reserve for garnish.

2. Discard all but 2 tablespoons drippings from Dutch oven. Stir in flour, salt, and ground red pepper and cook over medium heat, stirring frequently, about 5 minutes, until golden brown.

3. Stir in broth, fresh greens, spinach, potato, and water; heat to boiling over high heat. Reduce heat; cover and simmer, stirring occasionally, 20 to 24 minutes, until soup thickens slightly and greens are tender. To serve, sprinkle bacon over soup. Makes 10 cups or 8 first-course servings.

Each serving: About 145 calories, 7 g protein, 14 g carbohydrate, 7 g total fat (3 g saturated), 9 mg cholesterol, 735 mg sodium.

◆ *Clockwise from top left: Green Gumbo, Butternut Soup, and Cauliflower-Cheddar Soup*

BUTTERNUT SOUP

PREP: 45 MINUTES
COOK: 20 MINUTES

Cinnamon Croutons (see below)
1 medium leek
3 tablespoons butter or margarine
2 medium carrots, peeled and coarsely chopped
1 medium onion, coarsely chopped
1 medium butternut squash (2½ pounds), peeled
*   and cut into 1-inch pieces*
1 can (14½ ounces) chicken broth
½ teaspoon salt
2¼ cups water
½ cup half-and-half or light cream

1. Prepare Cinnamon Croutons.

2. Cut off root end from leek. Cut leek lengthwise in half; rinse with cold running water to remove sand. Coarsely chop white and pale-green part of leek; discard tough dark-green part.

3. In 5-quart Dutch oven or saucepot, melt butter over medium-high heat. Add carrots, onion, and leek and cook, stirring occasionally, about 10 minutes, until browned. Add squash, broth, salt, and water; heat to boiling. Reduce heat; cover and simmer 15 to 20 minutes, until squash is very tender.

4. In blender, with center part of cover removed to allow steam to escape, puree squash mixture in small batches until smooth. Pour pureed soup into large bowl after each batch.

5. Return soup to Dutch oven; stir in half-and-half. Heat soup, stirring occasionally, until hot. Serve with Cinnamon Croutons. Makes about 8¾ cups or 12 first-course servings.

CINNAMON CROUTONS: Preheat oven to 400°F. Cut ½ loaf (4 ounces) French bread into ¾-inch cubes (about 4 cups). In bowl, combine 3 tablespoons melted butter or margarine, ¼ teaspoon ground cinnamon, scant ⅛ teaspoon salt, and bread cubes; toss to coat. Spread bread cubes in 15 ½" by 10 ½" jelly-roll pan; bake 10 to 12 minutes, until golden.

Each serving of soup with croutons: About 150 calories, 3 g protein, 20 g carbohydrate, 7 g total fat (2 g saturated), 5 mg cholesterol, 355 mg sodium.

MUSHROOM AND WILD RICE SOUP

PREP: 45 MINUTES
COOK: 1 HOUR

½ cup wild rice
2½ cups plus 2 tablespoons water
1 package (½ ounce) dried mushrooms
2 cups boiling water
2 tablespoons olive oil
2 celery stalks, chopped
1 large onion, chopped
1 package (10 ounces) mushrooms, cut into
*   ¼-inch-thick slices*
2 cans (14½ ounces each) chicken broth
1 tablespoon soy sauce
½ teaspoon dried thyme
¼ teaspoon coarsely ground black pepper
¼ cup cream sherry

1. In 3-quart saucepan, heat wild rice and 2½ cups water to boiling over high heat. Reduce heat; cover and simmer 45 minutes, or until rice is tender and most of water has been absorbed.

2. Meanwhile, in 4-cup glass measuring cup, add dried mushrooms to 2 cups boiling water; set aside.

3. In nonstick 12-inch skillet, heat 1 tablespoon oil over medium heat. Add celery, onion, and 2 tablespoons water; cook about 10 minutes, until vegetables are tender and lightly browned. Transfer mixture to 4-quart saucepan.

4. In same skillet, heat remaining 1 tablespoon oil over medium-high heat. Add sliced mushrooms; cook about 10 minutes, until mushrooms are tender and lightly browned. Transfer to 4-quart saucepan with celery mixture.

5. With slotted spoon, remove dried mushrooms from soaking liquid and coarsely chop; strain liquid. Add dried mushrooms and their liquid to saucepan; stir in broth, soy sauce, thyme, pepper, and wild rice with any cooking liquid; heat to boiling over high heat. Stir in sherry. Reduce heat; cover and simmer 5 minutes. Makes about 9 cups or 8 first-course servings.

Each serving: About 130 calories, 5 g protein, 16 g carbohydrate, 4 g total fat (1 g saturated), 4 mg cholesterol, 430 mg sodium.

CHICKEN AND ESCAROLE SOUP WITH MEATBALLS

PREP: 1 HOUR
COOK: 1 HOUR 15 MINUTES

1 chicken (4 pounds), cut up
1 large onion, cut in half
¼ teaspoon whole black peppercorns
1 bay leaf
12 cups water
1 pound ground meat for meat loaf (ground beef, pork, and veal)
2 garlic cloves, crushed with garlic press
1 large egg, beaten
¼ cup chopped fresh flat-leaf parsley
½ teaspoon ground black pepper
¾ cup grated Romano cheese, plus additional for serving
2¾ teaspoons salt
1 cup plain dried bread crumbs
⅓ cup milk
1 can (14½ ounces) chicken broth
3 medium carrots, peeled and sliced
2 medium celery stalks, sliced
1 small head escarole (8 ounces), cut into ½-inch strips, with tough stems discarded

1. In 8-quart Dutch oven or saucepot, combine chicken, onion, peppercorns, bay leaf, and water; heat to boiling over high heat. Reduce heat; cover and simmer 1 hour 15 minutes, or until chicken is tender.

2. Meanwhile, prepare meatballs: In large bowl, with hands, combine ground meat, garlic, egg, parsley, pepper, ½ cup Romano cheese, and ¾ teaspoon salt. In small bowl with fork, mix bread crumbs and milk to form a thick paste. Mix bread-crumb mixture into meat mixture just until blended. Shape meat mixture into about seventy 1-inch meatballs (for easier shaping, use slightly wet hands) and place on cookie sheet; cover and refrigerate 30 minutes.

3. Transfer chicken to bowl; set aside until cool enough to handle. Discard skin and bones; cut chicken into bite-size pieces. Reserve 2 cups cut-up chicken; refrigerate remaining chicken for another use. Pour chicken broth through sieve lined with paper towels into large bowl. Let stand until fat separates from meat juice. Skim fat from broth and discard.

4. Return broth to clean Dutch oven or saucepot. Add canned broth and remaining 2 teaspoons salt; heat to boiling over high heat. Stir in carrots and celery; heat to boiling. Reduce heat; cover and simmer 8 to 10 minutes, until vegetables are tender. Add meatballs and remaining ¼ cup Romano cheese; heat to boiling over high heat. Reduce heat; cover and simmer 15 minutes, or until meatballs are cooked through. Stir in escarole and reserved chicken; heat through. Serve with grated Romano cheese to sprinkle over each serving. Makes about 16 cups or 14 first-course servings.

Each serving: About 235 calories, 18 g protein, 10 g carbohydrate, 13 g total fat (5 g saturated), 61 mg cholesterol, 760 mg sodium.

Entrees

ROAST TURKEY WITH PAN GRAVY

PREP: 45 MINUTES
ROAST: ABOUT 3 HOURS 45 MINUTES

1 fresh or frozen (thawed) turkey (14 pounds)
2 teaspoons salt
½ teaspoon coarsely ground black pepper
2 tablespoons all-purpose flour
fresh herbs and grapes for garnish

1. Preheat oven to 325°F. Remove giblets and neck from turkey; reserve for making pan gravy. Rinse turkey with cold running water and drain well.

2. Fasten neck skin to back with 1 or 2 skewers. With turkey breast side up, fold wings under back of turkey so they stay in place. Depending on brand of turkey, with string, tie legs and tail together, or push drumsticks under band of skin, or use stuffing clamp.

3. Place turkey, breast side up, on rack in large roasting pan (17" by 11½"). Rub turkey all over with 1½ teaspoons salt and pepper. Cover turkey with a loose tent of foil. Roast about 3 hours 45 minutes; start checking for doneness during last hour of roasting.

4. While turkey is roasting, in 3-quart saucepan, combine gizzard, heart, neck, and enough *water* to cover and heat to boiling over high heat. Reduce heat; cover and simmer 45 minutes. Add liver and cook 15 minutes longer. Drain, reserving broth. Pull meat from neck; discard bones. Coarsely chop neck meat and giblets. Cover and refrigerate meat and broth separately.

5. To brown turkey, remove foil during last 1 hour of roasting time and baste occasionally with pan drippings. Turkey is done when temperature on meat thermometer inserted in thickest part of thigh next to body registers 180° to 185°F and drumstick feels soft when pressed with fingers protected by paper towels. (Breast temperature should be 170° to 175°F.)

6. When turkey is done, place on warm large platter; keep warm. Prepare pan gravy: Remove rack from roasting pan. Pour pan drippings through sieve into 4-cup measure or medium bowl. Add 1 cup giblet broth to roasting pan and stir until brown bits are loosened; pour into drippings in measuring cup. Let stand until fat separates from meat juice. Spoon 2 tablespoons fat from drippings into 2-quart saucepan; skim and discard any remaining fat. Add remaining giblet broth and enough *water* to meat juice in cup to equal 3 cups.

7. Into fat in saucepan, stir flour and remaining ½ teaspoon salt; cook, over medium heat, stirring, until flour turns golden brown. Gradually stir in meat-juice mixture and cook, stirring, until gravy boils and thickens slightly. Stir in reserved giblets and neck meat; heat through. Pour gravy into gravy boat. Makes 3 cups.

8. To serve, garnish with fresh herbs and grapes. Serve with gravy. Remove skin from turkey before eating, if you like. Makes 14 main-dish servings.

Each serving turkey without skin or gravy: About 330 calories, 57 g protein, 0 g carbohydrate, 10 g total fat (3 g saturated), 149 mg cholesterol, 250 mg sodium.

Each ¼ cup of gravy: About 65 calories, 7 g protein, 2 g carbohydrate, 4 g total fat (1 g saturated) 63 mg cholesterol, 110 mg sodium.

◆ *Roast Turkey with Pan Gravy*

PORK CROWN ROAST
WITH APPLE STUFFING

PREP: 30 MINUTES
ROAST: ABOUT 2 HOURS

1 pork rib crown roast (7 pounds), well trimmed

2 ¼ teaspoons salt

½ plus ⅛ teaspoon ground black pepper

6 tablespoons butter or margarine

4 medium celery stalks, finely chopped

1 large onion, finely chopped

3 large Golden Delicious apples (1 ½ pounds),
    peeled, cored, and finely chopped

12 slices firm white bread, cut into ½-inch pieces
    (about 8 cups)

½ cup apple juice

1 teaspoon poultry seasoning

1 large egg

¼ cup applejack brandy, Calvados, or apple juice

3 tablespoons all-purpose flour

1 can (14 ½ ounces) chicken broth

kale and small apples for garnish

1. Preheat oven to 325°F. Rub inside and outside of pork roast with 1 teaspoon salt and ¼ teaspoon pepper. Place pork, rib ends down, in large roasting pan (17" by 11 ½"). Roast pork 1 hour.

2. Meanwhile, in 5-quart Dutch oven, melt butter over medium heat. Add celery and onion and cook, stirring often, about 10 minutes, until tender. Add apples and cook 6 to 8 minutes longer, until tender. Remove from heat; stir in bread pieces, apple juice, poultry seasoning, egg, 1 teaspoon salt, and ¼ teaspoon pepper.

3. When pork has roasted 1 hour, remove from oven and turn rib ends up. Spoon about 4 cups stuffing into cavity. (Place remaining stuffing in greased 1 ½-quart casserole; bake, uncovered, during last 30 minutes of pork roasting time.)

4. Return pork to oven and continue roasting about 1 hour longer, until meat thermometer inserted between 2 ribs into thickest part of meat registers 155°F. Internal temperature of meat will rise to 160°F upon standing. If stuffing browns too quickly during roasting, cover it loosely with foil.

5. When roast is done, transfer to warm large platter; let stand 15 minutes to set juices for easier slicing.

6. Meanwhile, prepare gravy: Pour pan drippings into 2-cup measuring cup or medium bowl; set pan aside. Let stand until fat separates from meat juice. Spoon 3 tablespoons fat from drippings (add enough melted butter, if necessary, to equal 3 tablespoons) into 2-quart saucepan; skim and discard any remaining fat. Add applejack to roasting pan and stir until brown bits are loosened; add to meat juice in cup.

7. Into drippings in saucepan, stir flour, remaining ¼ teaspoon salt and ⅛ teaspoon pepper; cook over medium heat, stirring, 1 minute. Gradually stir in meat-juice mixture and broth and cook, stirring, until gravy boils and thickens. Makes about 2 ½ cups.

8. To serve, garnish with kale and apples. Serve pork with gravy and stuffing. Makes 14 main-dish servings.

Each serving pork with stuffing: About 480 calories, 35 g protein, 18 g carbohydrate, 30 g total fat (10 g saturated), 95 mg cholesterol, 565 mg sodium.

Each tablespoon gravy: About 15 calories, 0 g protein, 1 g carbohydrate, 1 g total fat (0 g saturated), 1 mg cholesterol, 50 mg sodium.

◆ *Pork Crown Roast with
Apple Stuffing*

APPLE GINGER-GLAZED HAM

PREP: 15 MINUTES
COOK: 3 TO 3 HOURS 30 MINUTES

1 fully cooked smoked whole ham (14 pounds)
½ cup apple jelly
¼ teaspoon ground ginger
fresh herbs for garnish

1. Preheat oven to 325°F. Remove skin and trim some fat from ham, leaving about ¼-inch fat covering.

2. Place ham on rack in large roasting pan (17" by 11½"). Bake ham 2 hours 30 minutes.

3. After ham has baked 2 hours 30 minutes, prepare glaze: In small saucepan, combine apple jelly and ginger and heat to boiling over medium-high heat; boil 2 minutes. Brush ham with some glaze. Bake ham 30 minutes to 1 hour longer, brushing occasionally with remaining glaze, until meat thermometer inserted into center of ham registers 140°F (15 to 18 minutes per pound total cooking time).

4. When ham is done, transfer to warm large platter; let stand 20 minutes to set juices for easier slicing. Garnish with herbs. Makes 20 main-dish servings.

Each serving: About 175 calories, 30 g protein, 10 g carbohydrate, 5 g total fat (2 g saturated), 81 mg cholesterol, 1500 mg sodium.

◆ *Apple-Ginger Glazed Ham*

◆ *Beef Rib Roast with Creamy*
Horseradish Sauce

BEEF RIB ROAST
WITH CREAMY HORSERADISH SAUCE

PREP: 15 MINUTES
ROAST: 3 HOURS

1 (3-rib) beef rib roast, small end (about
7 pounds), chine bone removed
3 tablespoons whole tricolor peppercorns (red, green,
and black)
1 teaspoon salt
Creamy Horseradish Sauce (see below)

1. Preheat oven to 325°F. In medium roasting pan
(14" by 10"), place beef roast, fat side up. In mortar
with pestle, crush peppercorns with salt. Rub pepper-
corn mixture over roast.

2. Roast beef until meat thermometer inserted into
center registers 140°F (about 20 minutes per pound).
Internal temperature will rise to 145°F (medium)
upon standing. Or, roast to desired doneness.

3. When beef is done, transfer to warm large platter
and let stand 15 minutes to set juices for easier slicing. Meanwhile, prepare Creamy Horseradish Sauce.
Makes 10 main-dish servings.

Each serving: About 410 calories, 35 g protein, 1 g
carbohydrate, 29 g total fat (12 g saturated), 97 mg
cholesterol, 295 mg sodium

CREAMY HORSERADISH SAUCE: In small bowl,
mix 1 jar (6 ounces) prepared white horseradish,
drained, ½ cup mayonnaise, 1 teaspoon sugar, and ½
teaspoon salt. Whip ½ cup heavy or whipping cream;
fold into horseradish mixture. Makes about 1⅔ cups.

Each tablespoon: About 50 calories, 0 g protein, 1 g
carbohydrate, 5 g total fat (2 g saturated), 8 mg cholesterol, 70 mg sodium.

CRISPY CITRUS GOOSE

PREP: 30 MINUTES
ROAST: ABOUT 4 HOURS 30 MINUTES

1 fresh or frozen (thawed) goose (12 pounds)
1 bunch fresh thyme
4 bay leaves
5 medium oranges, each cut in half
½ teaspoon coarsely ground black pepper
½ teaspoon dried thyme
1 ¼ teaspoons salt
2 tablespoons cornstarch
3 tablespoons orange-flavored liqueur
½ cup orange marmalade
orange wedges and thyme sprigs for garnish

1. Preheat oven to 400°F. Remove giblets and neck from goose; refrigerate or freeze for another use. Discard fat from body cavity and any excess skin. Rinse goose with cold running water and drain well.
2. With breast side up, fold wings under back so they stay in place. Place thyme sprigs, bay leaves, and 6 orange halves in body cavity. With string, tie legs and tail together. Fold neck skin over back.
3. Place goose, breast side up, on rack in large roasting pan (17" by 11½"). With fork, prick skin in many places. In cup, mix pepper, dried thyme, and 1 teaspoon salt; rub mixture over goose.
4. Cover roasting pan with foil and roast goose 1 hour 30 minutes. Turn oven control to 325°F, and roast goose 2 hours longer.
5. Meanwhile, from remaining 4 orange halves squeeze ¾ cup juice. Stir in cornstarch, 1 tablespoon

◆ *Crispy Citrus Goose*

orange-flavored liqueur, and remaining ¼ teaspoon salt; set aside. In cup, mix orange marmalade with remaining 2 tablespoons orange-flavored liqueur.
6. Remove foil and roast goose 45 minutes longer. Remove goose from oven and turn oven control to 450°F. With spoon or bulb baster, remove as much fat as possible from pan into 8-cup glass measure or large bowl. Brush orange-marmalade mixture over goose. Roast goose 10 minutes longer, or until skin is golden and crisp. Goose is done when temperature on meat thermometer inserted into thickest part of meat between breast and thigh, registers 180° to 185°F and juices run clear when thickest part of thigh is pierced with tip of knife.
7. Transfer goose to warm large platter; let stand 10 minutes to set juices for easier slicing. Prepare sauce: Remove rack from roasting pan. Pour remaining pan drippings through sieve into 8-cup glass measure. Let stand until fat separates from meat juice; pour off and discard fat (there should be about 5 cups fat and 1 cup meat juice; if necessary, add enough *water* to meat juice to equal 1 cup). Return meat juice to pan and add reserved orange-juice mixture. Heat sauce mixture to boiling over medium heat; boil 30 seconds.
8. To serve, garnish platter with orange wedges and thyme sprigs. Pour orange sauce into gravy boat. Makes 10 main-dish servings.

Each serving of goose without skin: About 460 calories, 50 g protein, 12 g carbohydrate, 25 g total fat (8 g saturated), 170 mg cholesterol, 345 mg sodium.

Each tablespoon sauce: About 5 calories, 0 g protein, 1 g carbohydrate, 0 g total fat (0 g saturated), 0 mg cholesterol, 20 mg sodium.

Tarragon-Roasted Salmon
with Caper Sauce

PREP: 20 MINUTES
ROAST: ABOUT 40 MINUTES

Caper Sauce

¾ cup sour cream
½ cup mayonnaise
¼ cup milk
3 tablespoons capers, drained and chopped
2 tablespoons chopped fresh tarragon
½ teaspoon grated lemon peel
⅛ teaspoon ground black pepper

Salmon

2 large lemons, thinly sliced
1 whole salmon (5 ½ pounds), cleaned and
    scaled, with head and tail removed
2 tablespoons olive oil
½ teaspoon salt
½ teaspoon coarsely ground black pepper
1 large bunch fresh tarragon
1 small bunch fresh flat-leaf parsley
lemon wedges and tarragon sprigs for garnish

1. Prepare caper sauce: In medium bowl, with fork, mix all sauce ingredients until blended. Cover and refrigerate up to 2 days or until ready to serve. Makes about 1⅓ cups.

2. Prepare salmon: Preheat oven to 450°F. Line 15 ½" by 10 ½" jelly-roll pan with foil.

3. Place one-third of lemon slices in a row down center of pan. Rub outside of salmon with oil. Place salmon on top of lemon slices. Sprinkle cavity with salt and pepper. Place tarragon and parsley sprigs inside cavity along with half of remaining lemon slices. Place remaining lemon slices on top of fish.

4. Roast salmon about 40 minutes, until fish turns opaque throughout and flakes easily when tested with a fork. Remove lemon slices and skin from top of salmon; discard. Transfer salmon to warm large platter. Garnish with lemon wedges and tarragon sprigs. Serve with caper sauce. Makes 10 main-dish servings.

Each serving fish without sauce: About 180 calories, 25 g protein, 0 g carbohydrate, 8 g total fat (2 g saturated), 45 mg cholesterol, 160 mg sodium.

Each tablespoon sauce: About 60 calories, 0 g protein, 1 g carbohydrate, 6 g total fat (2 g saturated), 6 mg cholesterol, 80 mg sodium.

◆ *Tarragon-Roasted Salmon*
with Caper Sauce

◆ *To serve a whole fish as elegantly as any restaurant, peel off the top skin with a fork and knife. Slide the knife under the front section of fillet and, using a wide spatula, transfer the top fillet to a long platter. Slide the knife under the backbone and lift it away from the bottom fillet. Slide the knife between the bottom skin and fillet and transfer the fillet to the platter.*

Side Dishes

GREEN BEANS WITH HONEY-PECAN BUTTER

PREP: 30 MINUTES PLUS CHILLING OR FREEZING
COOK: ABOUT 12 MINUTES

½ cup pecans
½ cup butter or margarine, softened
2 tablespoons honey
½ teaspoon coarsely ground black pepper
2 pounds green beans, trimmed

1. Preheat oven to 375°F. Place nuts in 8" by 8" metal baking pan. Bake 8 to 10 minutes, until lightly toasted. Cool completely. In food processor, with knife blade attached, process pecans until finely ground.
2. In bowl, with spoon, mix butter with honey, pepper, and ground pecans until blended. Spoon mixture into a 6-inch-long strip across width of sheet of plastic wrap or waxed paper. Freeze about 20 minutes, until slightly firm. Roll mixture, covered with plastic wrap or waxed paper, back and forth, to make a 6-inch-long log. Wrap well; refrigerate up to 2 days or freeze up to 2 months (thaw in refrigerator 1 hour before using).
3. In 12-inch skillet, heat *½ inch water* and green beans to boiling over high heat. Reduce heat; simmer 5 to 10 minutes, until beans are just tender-crisp. Drain; rinse with cold running water to stop cooking. Transfer beans to zip-tight plastic bag and refrigerate up to 2 days if not serving right away.
4. To serve, in 12-inch skillet, heat cooked beans with one-fourth of pecan butter over medium heat until butter melts and beans are hot. Makes 8 accompaniment servings.

Each serving: About 75 calories, 2 g protein, 9 g carbohydrate, 4 g total fat (1 g saturated), 0 mg cholesterol, 40 mg sodium.

SPICY PEARL ONIONS

PREP: 45 MINUTES
COOK: ABOUT 20 MINUTES

3 baskets (10 ounces each) pearl onions
3 tablespoons dark brown sugar
2 tablespoons butter or margarine
2 teaspoons raspberry vinegar
1 teaspoon tomato paste
¼ teaspoon salt
¼ teaspoon ground red pepper (cayenne) or
* 1 teaspoon chipotle chile puree*

1. In deep 12-inch skillet, heat *1 inch water* to boiling over high heat. Add onions; heat to boiling. Reduce heat; cover and simmer 5 to 10 minutes, until onions are tender. Drain well. Wipe skillet dry.
2. Peel onions, leaving a little of the root ends to help hold their shape during glazing. Let onions cool slightly; cover and refrigerate up to 24 hours, if not serving right away.
3. To serve, in 12-inch skillet, combine brown sugar and remaining ingredients and heat over high heat, stirring often, until melted. Add onions and cook, stirring occasionally, about 10 minutes, until onions are browned and glazed. Makes 8 accompaniment servings.

Each serving: About 85 calories, 1 g protein, 14 g carbohydrate, 3 g total fat (1 g saturated), 0 mg cholesterol, 120 mg sodium.

◆ *Spicy Pearl Onions and*
Green Beans with Honey-Pecan Butter

◆ *Braised Celery*

ring, 1 minute longer. Stir in broth and water; heat to boiling. Stir in celery, spooning vegetable mixture over celery; heat to boiling. Reduce heat; cover and simmer 40 to 45 minutes, until celery is very tender and most of liquid has evaporated. Transfer to serving bowl; or cover and refrigerate up to 24 hours if not serving immediately.

3. To serve, return celery mixture to skillet and cook over medium heat about 10 minutes, until heated through. Makes 6 accompaniment servings.

Each serving: About 90 calories, 2 g protein, 7 g carbohydrate, 7 g total fat (2 g saturated), 5 mg cholesterol, 245 mg sodium.

BRAISED CELERY

PREP: 20 MINUTES
COOK: 45 TO 55 MINUTES

1 bunch celery
1 tablespoon butter or margarine
2 slices bacon, finely chopped
1 small onion, finely chopped
1 small carrot, peeled and finely chopped
1 garlic clove, finely chopped
1 tablespoon tomato paste
½ cup chicken broth
½ cup water

1. Trim ends of celery stalks. With paring knife or vegetable peeler, remove tough strings from stalks. Cut stalks crosswise into thirds.
2. In 12-inch skillet, melt butter with bacon over medium heat. Stir in onion and carrot and cook 8 minutes, or until vegetables are tender. Stir in garlic and cook 30 seconds. Add tomato paste and cook, stir-

GREEN BEANS WITH TOASTED BENNE SEEDS

PREP: 25 MINUTES
COOK: 20 MINUTES

3 tablespoons lemon juice
1 tablespoon plus 1 teaspoon Dijon mustard
1 teaspoon salt
¼ cup olive oil
4 pounds green beans, trimmed
2 tablespoons sesame seeds (benne seeds), toasted

1. Prepare dressing: In small bowl, with wire whisk or fork, mix lemon juice, mustard, and salt until blended. In thin, steady stream, gradually whisk in oil.
2. In 8-quart Dutch oven, heat *1 inch water* to boiling over high heat. Add half of green beans and heat to boiling. Reduce heat; cover and simmer 5 to 10 minutes, until beans are just tender-crisp. Transfer beans to colander; drain well. Repeat with remaining beans.
3. In large bowl, toss warm beans with dressing; cover and refrigerate until ready to serve. Toss beans with sesame seeds just before serving. Makes 20 accompaniment servings.

Each serving: About 60 calories, 2 g protein, 7 g carbohydrate, 3 g total fat (0 g saturated), 0 mg cholesterol, 135 mg sodium.

APRICOT-GINGER CARROTS

PREP: 10 MINUTES
COOK: ABOUT 30 MINUTES

> 2 bags (16 ounces each) peeled baby carrots
> 2 tablespoons butter or margarine
> 2 green onions, finely chopped
> 1 large garlic clove, finely chopped
> 1 tablespoon minced, peeled fresh ginger
> 1/3 cup apricot jam
> 1 tablespoon balsamic vinegar
> 1/4 teaspoon salt
> pinch ground red pepper (cayenne)

1. Place steamer basket in deep 12-inch skillet with *1 inch water*; heat to boiling over high heat. Add carrots and reduce heat to medium; cover and cook 10 to 12 minutes, just until carrots are tender-crisp. Remove carrots and rinse with cold running water to stop cooking; drain well. Place carrots in large zip-tight plastic bag; refrigerate until ready to serve.

2. In 12-inch skillet, melt butter over medium heat. Add green onions, garlic, and ginger, and cook, stirring often, about 3 minutes, until tender. Add apricot jam, vinegar, salt, and ground red pepper and cook, stirring often, 3 to 4 minutes longer. Let glaze cool slightly. Pour glaze into small container; cover and refrigerate until ready to serve.

3. To serve, in 12-inch skillet, cook glaze and carrots over medium-high heat 5 minutes. Increase heat to high and cook, stirring occasionally, 3 minutes, or until carrots are well coated and heated through. Makes 8 accompaniment servings.

Each serving: About 115 calories, 1 g protein, 22 g carbohydrate, 3 g total fat (1 g saturated), 0 mg cholesterol, 145 mg sodium.

BRUSSELS SPROUTS WITH BACON

PREP: 15 MINUTES
COOK: 15 MINUTES

> 3 containers (10 ounces each) Brussels sprouts, trimmed
> 6 slices bacon
> 1 tablespoon olive oil
> 2 garlic cloves, crushed with garlic press
> 1/2 teaspoon salt
> 1/4 teaspoon coarsely ground black pepper
> 1/4 cup pine nuts (pignoli), toasted

1. In 4-quart saucepan, heat *1 inch water* to boiling over high heat. Add Brussels sprouts; heat to boiling. Reduce heat; cover and simmer 5 minutes, or until Brussels sprouts are tender-crisp. Drain. (If you like, Brussels sprouts can be cooked a day ahead. After draining, rinse with cold water to stop cooking; cover and refrigerate until ready to stir-fry in step 3.)

2. In nonstick 12-inch skillet, cook bacon over medium-low heat until browned. Transfer bacon to paper towels to drain; crumble.

3. Pour off all but 1 tablespoon drippings from skillet. Add oil and heat over medium-high heat. Add Brussels sprouts, garlic, salt, and pepper. Cook, stirring frequently, about 5 minutes, until Brussels sprouts are browned. Top with pine nuts and crumbled bacon. Makes 8 accompaniment servings.

Each serving: About 120 calories, 6 g protein, 10 g carbohydrate, 8 g total fat (2 g saturated), 6 mg cholesterol, 235 mg sodium.

SAUTÉED CABBAGE WITH PEAS

PREP: 10 MINUTES
COOK: ABOUT 40 MINUTES

2 tablespoons butter or margarine
1 medium onion, thinly sliced
1 small head savoy cabbage (2 pounds), cored and
    cut into ½-inch-thick slices, with tough
    ribs discarded
¾ teaspoon salt
½ teaspoon sugar
¼ teaspoon coarsely ground black pepper
½ cup chicken broth
1 package (10 ounces) frozen baby peas
¼ cup chopped fresh dill

1. In 12-inch skillet, melt butter over medium heat. Add onion and cook, stirring often, about 8 minutes, until tender and golden.

2. Add cabbage, salt, sugar, and pepper and cook, stirring often, about 5 minutes, until cabbage is tender-crisp. Stir in broth and cook cabbage mixture 10 minutes longer, or until cabbage is tender. Spoon cabbage mixture into bowl; cover and refrigerate up to 24 hours, if not serving right away.

3. To serve, return cabbage mixture to skillet; add frozen peas and dill. Cook over medium heat, stirring frequently, 12 to 15 minutes, until heated through. Makes 8 accompaniment servings.

Each serving: About 90 calories, 4 g protein, 13 g carbohydrate, 3 g total fat (1 g saturated), 0 mg cholesterol, 345 mg sodium.

◆ *Sautéed Cabbage with Peas and Mashed Root Vegetables*

MASHED ROOT VEGETABLES

PREP: 15 MINUTES
COOK: 25 MINUTES
BAKE: ABOUT 30 MINUTES

2 pounds assorted root vegetables (carrots, celery
    root {celeriac}, parsnips, white turnips, and/or
    rutabaga), peeled and cut into 1-inch pieces
    (5 cups)
1 pound all-purpose potatoes, peeled and cut into
    1-inch pieces (2½ to 3 cups)
2½ teaspoons salt
3 tablespoons butter or margarine
¼ teaspoon ground black pepper
pinch nutmeg

1. In 5- or 6-quart saucepot, combine root vegetables, potatoes, 2 teaspoons salt, and enough *water* to cover; heat to boiling over high heat. Reduce heat to medium and cook 15 minutes, or until vegetables and potatoes are tender. Drain.

2. Return vegetables to saucepot; add butter, pepper, and ½ teaspoon salt and mash with potato masher until smooth. Spoon mixture into 1½-quart casserole; cool slightly.

3. To serve, preheat oven to 350°F. Cover casserole and bake 30 minutes, or until heated through. Sprinkle with nutmeg. Makes 8 accompaniment servings.

Each serving: About 150 calories, 3 g protein, 26 g carbohydrate, 5 g total fat (1 g saturated), 0 mg cholesterol, 305 mg sodium.

◆ *Menu planning is a talent to be nurtured. An inspiring choice of side dishes, mixed and matched with your entree, should provide variety in color, texture, and taste. Try some of the more unusual cabbages and root vegetables; they're extremely rich in nutrients and delicious too!*

◆ *Wild Rice and Orzo Pilaf and Leeks Vinaigrette*

WILD RICE AND ORZO PILAF

PREP: 25 MINUTES
COOK: 55 MINUTES
BAKE: 45 MINUTES

1¼ cups orzo pasta (about 8 ounces)
1 cup wild rice (about 6 ounces)
3 tablespoons butter or margarine
1 small onion, finely chopped
1 medium celery stalk, finely chopped
1 pound medium mushrooms, trimmed and sliced
2 teaspoons chopped fresh thyme
1 teaspoon salt
¼ teaspoon coarsely ground black pepper
thyme sprigs for garnish

1. Prepare orzo and wild rice, separately, as labels direct.

2. Meanwhile, in 12-inch skillet, melt butter over medium heat. Add onion and celery and cook, stirring occasionally, about 10 minutes, until tender. Add mushrooms, thyme, salt, and pepper and cook, stirring occasionally, 10 minutes longer, or until mushrooms are tender and liquid has evaporated.

3. In shallow 2½-quart baking dish, combine orzo, rice, and mushroom mixture and stir until blended. Cool slightly. Cover and refrigerate up to 2 days, if not serving right away.

4. To serve, preheat oven to 350°F. Cover orzo mixture and bake, 45 minutes, or until hot. Makes about 9 cups or 12 accompaniment servings.

Each serving: About 155 calories, 5 g protein, 26 g carbohydrate, 3 g total fat (1 g saturated), 0 mg cholesterol, 220 mg sodium.

LEEKS VINAIGRETTE

PREP: 20 MINUTES
COOK: 10 MINUTES

16 slender leeks (4½ to 5 pounds)
2¼ teaspoons salt
2 tablespoons red wine vinegar
2 teaspoons Dijon mustard
¼ teaspoon ground black pepper
¼ cup olive oil
2 tablespoons chopped fresh parsley

1. In 8-quart Dutch oven, heat *5 quarts water* to boiling over high heat. Meanwhile, cut root ends from leeks. Trim leeks to 6 inches; discard tops (or save for another use). Cut leeks lengthwise almost in half down to beginning of white part, keeping bottom 2 to 3 inches intact. Remove any bruised or tough dark-green outer leaves. Rinse leeks thoroughly with cold running water, fanning cut part, to remove all sand.

2. Add leeks and 2 teaspoons salt to Dutch oven; cook 10 minutes, or until tender when pierced with knife. With slotted spoon, transfer leeks to colander to drain; rinse with cold running water. Drain again and pat dry with paper towels.

3. Coarsely chop any loose pieces of leek and spread on platter; arrange leeks in a row, in a single layer, on top. Cover leeks and refrigerate up to 24 hours, if not serving right away.

4. Prepare vinaigrette: In small bowl, with wire whisk or fork, mix vinegar, mustard, pepper, and remaining ¼ teaspoon salt until blended. In thin, steady stream, gradually whisk in oil. Pour vinaigrette into small jar; cover tightly and refrigerate until ready to serve.

5. Serve leeks at room temperature. Spoon vinaigrette evenly over leeks; sprinkle with parsley. Makes 8 accompaniment servings.

Each serving: About 105 calories, 1 g protein, 11 g carbohydrate, 7 g total fat (1 g saturated), 0 mg cholesterol, 180 mg sodium.

MASHED POTATOES WITH SAUERKRAUT

PREP: 15 MINUTES
COOK: 40 TO 45 MINUTES

SAUERKRAUT TOPPING

4 tablespoons butter or margarine
4 medium onions, thinly sliced
2 packages (16 ounces each) sauerkraut, rinsed and squeezed dry
1 can (14½ ounces) chicken broth
2 medium Golden Delicious apples, peeled, cored, and grated
½ teaspoon caraway seeds

MASHED POTATOES

15 medium all-purpose potatoes (5 pounds), peeled and cut into 1-inch chunks
1¼ teaspoons salt
1¼ cups milk, warmed
½ cup butter or margarine (1 stick)

1. Prepare topping: In 12-inch skillet, melt butter over medium heat. Add onions and cook, stirring occasionally, about 15 minutes, until tender and lightly browned. Add sauerkraut, broth, apples, and caraway seeds; heat to boiling over high heat. Reduce heat; cover and simmer 40 to 45 minutes, until sauerkraut is tender. Keep warm.

2. Meanwhile, prepare mashed potatoes: In 8-quart Dutch oven, combine potatoes and enough *water* to cover; heat to boiling over high heat. Reduce heat; cover and simmer 15 minutes, or until potatoes are fork-tender. Drain.

3. Return potatoes to Dutch oven. With potato masher, mash potatoes with salt. Add warmed milk and butter; mash until mixture is well blended. Spoon potatoes into serving bowl; top with sauerkraut. Makes 14 accompaniment servings.

Each serving: About 245 calories, 5 g protein, 34 g carbohydrate, 11 g total fat (2 g saturated), 3 mg cholesterol, 610 mg sodium.

◆ *Spinach and Potato Gratin*

1. Preheat oven to 350°F. Grease shallow 3-quart casserole.

2. In 10-inch skillet, melt butter over medium heat. Add shallots and cook, stirring occasionally, 5 minutes, or until tender. Remove skillet from heat; stir in spinach, nutmeg, ¼ teaspoon salt, and ¼ teaspoon pepper.

3. Arrange one-third of potato slices, overlapping, in casserole. Top with one-third of cheese and one-half of spinach mixture. Repeat layering with remaining ingredients, ending with cheese.

4. In 4-cup measuring cup or large bowl, with wire whisk, mix milk, cream, cornstarch, remaining ¾ teaspoon salt, and ¼ teaspoon pepper until smooth. Pour milk mixture evenly over casserole.

5. Place sheet of foil underneath casserole; crimp foil edges to form a rim to catch any overflow during baking. Cover and bake 30 minutes. Remove cover and bake 1 hour longer, or until center is hot and bubbly and top is golden. Makes 12 accompaniment servings.

Each serving: About 230 calories, 8 g protein, 24 g carbohydrate, 13 g total fat (7 g saturated), 42 mg cholesterol, 315 mg sodium.

SPINACH AND POTATO GRATIN

PREP: 40 MINUTES
BAKE: 1 HOUR 30 MINUTES

1 tablespoon butter or margarine

3 large shallots, thinly sliced

2 packages (10 ounces each) frozen chopped spinach, thawed and squeezed dry

⅛ teaspoon ground nutmeg

1 teaspoon salt

½ teaspoon coarsely ground black pepper

9 medium all-purpose potatoes (3 pounds), peeled and cut into ¼-inch-thick slices

4 ounces Gruyère cheese, shredded (1 cup)

1½ cups milk

1 cup heavy or whipping cream

1 tablespoon cornstarch

ROASTED RED AND WHITE POTATOES WITH GARLIC

PREP: 15 MINUTES
ROAST: 1 HOUR 25 MINUTES

4½ pounds medium red and all-purpose potatoes, unpeeled and each cut into quarters

2 medium red onions, each cut into 6 wedges

¼ cup olive oil

1¼ teaspoons salt

1 teaspoon dried thyme

½ teaspoon coarsely ground black pepper

2 garlic cloves, crushed with garlic press

fresh thyme sprigs for garnish

1. Preheat oven to 325°F. Place potatoes and red onions in large roasting pan (17" by 11½"). Add oil, salt, thyme, pepper, and garlic and toss to coat evenly. Roast 1 hour on lower rack of oven.

2. Turn oven control to 450°F and roast potatoes, turning occasionally with spatula, 25 minutes longer, until golden and fork-tender. Garnish with fresh thyme sprigs. Makes 10 accompaniment servings.

Each serving: About 210 calories, 5 g protein, 36 g carbohydrate, 6 g total fat (1 g saturated), 0 mg cholesterol, 280 mg sodium.

SWEET POTATO AND APPLE GRATIN

PREP: 40 MINUTES
BAKE: 1 HOUR

SWEET-POTATO LAYERS

2 tablespoons butter or margarine
3 large Golden Delicious apples (1 ¼ pounds), peeled, cored, and cut into ¼-inch-thick slices
1 large onion (12 ounces), cut in half and thinly sliced
2 tablespoons applejack brandy or Calvados
6 medium sweet potatoes (2 ½ pounds)
¾ teaspoon salt
¼ teaspoon coarsely ground black pepper
¼ teaspoon ground nutmeg
1 cup apple cider or apple juice

PECAN-CRUMB TOPPING

2 tablespoons butter or margarine
3 slices firm white bread, cut into ¼-inch pieces (1 ¾ cups)
½ cup pecans, coarsely chopped

1. Prepare sweet-potato layers: Grease shallow 2½-quart casserole. In 12-inch skillet, melt butter over medium heat. Add apples and onion and cook, stirring frequently, about 25 minutes, until tender and golden. Stir in applejack; cook 1 minute. Remove skillet from heat.

2. Meanwhile, peel and thinly slice sweet potatoes. In cup, mix salt, pepper, and nutmeg.

3. Arrange one-third of sweet potato slices, overlapping, in casserole. Spoon one-third of apple mixture over potatoes. Sprinkle with one-third salt mixture. Repeat layering 2 more times. Pour apple cider over potato and apple layers. Cover with foil and refrigerate up to 24 hours, if not serving right away.

4. Prepare topping: In nonstick 10-inch skillet, melt butter over medium heat. Add bread pieces and pecans and cook, stirring occasionally, 5 to 6 minutes, until bread and pecans are lightly toasted. Cool topping completely. Transfer topping to small container; cover and set aside, up to 24 hours.

5. To serve, preheat oven to 400°F. Cover casserole with foil and bake 1 hour. Remove foil; sprinkle casserole with topping just before serving. Makes 8 accompaniment servings.

Each serving: About 300 calories, 4 g protein, 50 g carbohydrate, 11 g total fat (2 g saturated), 0 mg cholesterol, 335 mg sodium.

◆ *Sweet Potato and Apple Gratin*

HOPPIN' JOHN

PREP: 15 MINUTES
COOK: 20 MINUTES

1 tablespoon vegetable oil
2 celery stalks, chopped
1 large onion, chopped
1 medium red pepper, chopped
2 garlic cloves, finely chopped
1 package (16 ounces) dried black-eyed peas
1 large smoked ham hock (¾ pound)
2 cans (14½ ounces each) chicken broth
¼ teaspoon crushed red pepper
1 bay leaf
2 teaspoons salt
4 cups water
2 cups regular long-grain rice
chopped parsley for garnish (optional)

1. In 4-quart saucepan, heat oil over medium-high heat. Add celery, onion, and red pepper; cook 10 minutes, or until golden. Add garlic; cook 2 minutes longer.

2. Rinse peas with cold running water and discard any stones or shriveled peas. Add peas, ham hock, broth, crushed red pepper, bay leaf, 1 teaspoon salt, and water to celery mixture; heat to boiling over high heat. Reduce heat; cover and simmer 40 minutes, or until peas are tender.

3. Meanwhile, prepare rice as label directs, but use remaining 1 teaspoon salt and do not add butter.

4. In large bowl, gently mix pea mixture and rice. Serve hot. Garnish with chopped parsley, if you like. Makes 20 accompaniment servings.

Each serving: About 150 calories, 8 g protein, 26 g carbohydrate, 2 g total fat (0 g saturated), 9 mg cholesterol, 455 mg sodium.

NEW ENGLAND APPLE-NUT STUFFING

PREP: 45 MINUTES
BAKE: 45 MINUTES

½ cup butter or margarine (1 stick)
3 large celery stalks, finely chopped
1 large onion, chopped
3 medium Golden Delicious apples (1 pound), peeled, cored, and finely chopped
1½ loaves (24 ounces) sliced firm white bread, cut into ¾-inch cubes and lightly toasted
1 can (14½ ounces) chicken broth
½ cup pecans, toasted and chopped
½ cup walnuts, toasted and chopped
2 tablespoons sesame seeds, toasted (optional)
½ teaspoon poultry seasoning
¼ teaspoon dried oregano leaves, crumbled
¼ teaspoon coarsely ground black pepper

1. Preheat oven to 325°F. In 12-inch skillet, melt butter over medium heat. Add celery and onion and cook, stirring occasionally, 10 minutes, or until tender. Add apples and cook 5 minutes longer.

2. In large bowl, combine celery mixture with toasted bread cubes and remaining ingredients; toss to mix well. Spoon stuffing into greased 13" by 9" glass baking dish; cover with foil and bake 45 minutes, or until heated through. Makes about 12 cups.

Each ½ cup: About 155 calories, 3 g protein, 18 g carbohydrate, 8 g total fat (1 g saturated), 0 mg cholesterol, 255 mg sodium.

ITALIAN SAUSAGE STUFFING

PREP: 25 MINUTES
BAKE: 30 MINUTES

> 1 pound sweet Italian-sausage links, casings
>   removed
> 1 package (14 to 16 ounces) herb-seasoned
>   stuffing mix
> ½ cup butter or margarine (1 stick)
> 2 large celery stalks, finely chopped
> 1 medium onion, finely chopped
> 2½ cups hot water

1. Preheat oven to 325°F. Heat 10-inch skillet over medium-high heat until hot. Add sausage and cook, stirring frequently to break up sausage, about 10 minutes, until browned. With slotted spoon, transfer sausage to large bowl; stir in stuffing mix.

◆ *Italian Sausage Stuffing*

2. To drippings in skillet, add butter; heat until melted. Add celery and onion and cook, stirring occasionally, about 10 minutes, until vegetables are tender and golden. Transfer celery mixture to bowl with sausage.
3. Pour hot water over stuffing mixture; toss to mix well. Spoon stuffing into 13" by 9" glass baking dish; cover with foil and bake 30 minutes, or until stuffing is heated through. Makes about 12 cups.

Each ½ cup: About 175 calories, 4 g protein, 16 g carbohydrate, 10 g total fat (3 g saturated), 15 mg cholesterol, 480 mg sodium.

DRIED APRICOT, PRUNE, AND CHERRY COMPOTE

PREP: 10 MINUTES PLUS COOLING
COOK: 8 MINUTES

> 4 cups apple cider or apple juice
> 8 ounces (1 cup) dried apricots, each cut into
>   3 strips
> ¼ cup packed light brown sugar
> 3 strips (3" by 1" each) lemon peel
> 1 cinnamon stick (3 inches)
> 8 ounces (1 cup) pitted prunes, each cut in half
> 4 ounces (½ cup) dried tart cherries
> ½ teaspoon vanilla extract

1. In 3-quart saucepan, combine apple cider, apricots, brown sugar, lemon peel, and cinnamon stick and heat to boiling over high heat. Reduce heat; simmer, uncovered, 5 minutes.
2. Spoon mixture into large bowl; stir in prunes, dried cherries, and vanilla. Serve at room temperature or cover with plastic wrap and refrigerate. Store in refrigerator up to 1 week. Makes 10 servings.

Each serving: About 175 calories, 2 g protein, 46 g carbohydrate, 1 g total fat (0 g saturated), 0 mg cholesterol, 7 mg sodium.

CRANBERRY-FIG CHUTNEY

PREP: 15 MINUTES PLUS CHILLING
COOK: 35 MINUTES

> 1 bag (12 ounces) cranberries (3 cups)
> 1 package (8-ounces) dried Calimyrna figs, sliced
> 1 small onion, chopped
> ½ small lemon, chopped
> 1 cup packed brown sugar
> ⅓ cup red wine vinegar
> 2 tablespoons minced, peeled fresh ginger
> ½ teaspoon salt
> ¼ teaspoon coarsely ground black pepper
> 1 cup water

In 3-quart saucepan, heat all ingredients to boiling over medium-high heat. Reduce heat; simmer, uncovered, stirring occasionally, 30 minutes. Cover and refrigerate chutney about 4 hours, until well chilled. If you like, transfer chutney to an airtight container and refrigerate up to 2 days. Makes about 4 cups.

Each ¼ cup: About 105 calories, 1 g protein, 27 g carbohydrate, 0 g total fat (0 g saturated), 0 mg cholesterol, 75 mg sodium.

CRANBERRY-PEAR RELISH

PREP: 5 MINUTES PLUS CHILLING
COOK: 12 TO 14 MINUTES

> 1 bag (12 ounces) cranberries (3 cups)
> 1 ¼ cups packed brown sugar
> ¼ cup balsamic vinegar
> ½ cup water
> 1 medium pear, peeled, cored, and finely chopped

In 3-quart saucepan, combine cranberries, sugar, vinegar, and water and heat to boiling over high heat, stirring occasionally. Reduce heat; simmer, uncovered, 8 minutes, or until most of cranberries have popped. Add pear; cover and cook 2 to 3 minutes longer. Cover and refrigerate relish about 4 hours, until well chilled. If you like, transfer relish to airtight container and refrigerate up to 2 days. Makes about 3 cups.

Each ¼ cup: About 115 calories, 0 g protein, 29 g carbohydrate, 0 g total fat (0 g saturated), 0 mg cholesterol, 10 mg sodium.

NO-COOK CRANBERRY-ORANGE RELISH

PREP: 15 MINUTES PLUS CHILLING

> 1 bag (12 ounces) cranberries (3 cups)
> 1 medium orange, cut up
> ½ cup dark seedless raisins
> ½ cup sugar

In food processor with knife blade attached, combine all ingredients and process until mixture is coarsely chopped. Cover and refrigerate relish about 2 hours, until well chilled. If you like, transfer relish to an airtight container and refrigerate up to 2 days. Makes about 3 cups.

Each ¼ cup: About 70 calories, 1 g protein, 18 g carbohydrate, 0 g total fat (0 g saturated), 0 mg cholesterol, 10 mg sodium.

◆ *From top: Cranberry-Fig Chutney, Cranberry-Pear Relish, and No-Cook Cranberry-Orange Relish*

◆ *Condiments really perk up the palate—their sharp, sweet, and savory flavors enliven many a dish. But with varied textures and glistening jewel-like colors, they're also a feast for the eyes.*

Salads

WINTER SALAD WITH RIPE PEARS AND TOASTED PECANS

PREP: 45 MINUTES

3 tablespoons red wine vinegar
2 teaspoons Dijon mustard
½ teaspoon salt
½ teaspoon coarsely ground black pepper
⅓ cup olive oil
3 medium, ripe pears, peeled, cored, and each cut into 16 wedges
1 wedge Parmesan cheese (4 ounces)
2 small heads radicchio (7 ounces each), torn into large pieces
2 small heads Belgian endive, separated into leaves
2 bunches arugula (4 ounces each), trimmed
½ cup pecans, toasted and coarsely chopped

1. In very large bowl, with wire whisk or fork, mix vinegar, mustard, salt, and pepper until blended. In thin, steady stream, gradually whisk in oil until mixture thickens slightly. Add pear wedges; toss to coat pears with dressing.
2. With vegetable peeler, shave 1 cup loosely packed shavings from wedge of Parmesan cheese; set aside.
3. Add radicchio, endive, and arugula to bowl with pears; toss to coat evenly. Serve salad topped with Parmesan shavings and pecans. Makes 10 accompaniment servings.

Each serving: About 205 calories, 7 g protein, 14 g carbohydrate, 15 g total fat (3 g saturated), 9 mg cholesterol, 360 mg sodium.

SPINACH AND TANGERINE SALAD

PREP: 30 MINUTES

4 medium tangerines or small oranges
1 large bunch (1 pound) spinach, tough stems trimmed
2 small heads Bibb lettuce (8 ounces)
3 tablespoons extra virgin olive oil
3 tablespoons cider vinegar
1 teaspoon sugar
1 teaspoon Dijon mustard
⅛ teaspoon salt
⅛ teaspoon coarsely ground black pepper

1. From 1 tangerine, grate peel. Cut remaining peel and pith from all tangerines; discard. Cut each tangerine in half, then cut each half crosswise into ¼-inch-thick slices. Tear spinach and Bibb lettuce into bite-size pieces.
2. In large bowl, with wire whisk or fork, mix oil, vinegar, sugar, mustard, salt, pepper, and tangerine peel. Add spinach, lettuce, and tangerine slices; toss well. Makes 8 first-course servings.

Each serving: About 80 calories, 2 g protein, 8 g carbohydrate, 5 g total fat (1 g saturated), 0 mg cholesterol, 95 mg sodium.

◆ *Washing greens is an easy do-ahead task. Tear into bite-size pieces by hand (a knife blade may bruise leaves), soak briefly, and spin or pat dry. Wrap in paper towels, then enclose in plastic bags. Place in your crisper. Use within two or three days.*

◆ *Beet, Orange, and Watercress Salad*

BEET, ORANGE, AND WATERCRESS SALAD

PREP: 45 MINUTES
COOK: 30 MINUTES

2 pounds beets without tops (10 medium beets)
4 large oranges
¼ cup red wine vinegar
1 tablespoon Dijon mustard
1 teaspoon sugar
¾ teaspoon salt
¼ teaspoon coarsely ground black pepper
¼ cup olive oil
3 bunches watercress (4 ounces each), tough stems discarded
1 medium red onion, thinly sliced

1. In 4-quart saucepan, heat beets and enough *water* to cover over high heat, to boiling. Reduce heat; cover and simmer 30 minutes, or until beets are fork-tender.
2. Meanwhile, from 1 orange, grate 1 teaspoon peel. Cut peel and white pith from all oranges. Holding oranges over large bowl to catch juice, cut out sections between membranes. Place sections in small bowl; set aside. Into juice, with wire whisk or fork, mix vinegar, mustard, sugar, salt, pepper, and orange peel until blended. In thin, steady stream, gradually whisk in oil.
3. Drain beets and cool with cold running water. Peel and cut each beet in half, then cut each half into ¼-inch-thick slices.
4. To dressing in bowl, add beets, orange sections, watercress, and red onion; toss to coat. Makes 10 accompaniment servings.

Each serving: About 110 calories, 3 g protein, 15 g carbohydrate, 6 g total fat (1 g saturated), 0 mg cholesterol, 250 mg sodium.

Holiday Brunch

BREAD PUDDING WITH WARM BANANA-MAPLE SAUCE

PREP: 20 MINUTES PLUS OVERNIGHT
BAKE: 45 MINUTES

> 1 loaf unsliced rich egg bread, such as challah
>   (1 pound), cut into 1-inch-thick slices
> 3 cups milk
> ½ teaspoon salt
> 10 large eggs
> ¼ cup plus 1 tablespoon sugar
> 1 teaspoon ground cinnamon
> 4 tablespoons butter or margarine
> 6 medium firm bananas, cut into ¼-inch-thick
>   slices
> 1 bottle (8 ounces) maple syrup

1. Grease shallow 3 ½- to 4-quart ceramic casserole or 13" by 9" glass baking dish. Arrange bread slices, overlapping slightly, in dish.

2. In medium bowl, with wire whisk or fork, beat milk, salt, eggs, and ¼ cup sugar until well mixed. Slowly pour egg mixture over bread slices; prick bread slices with fork and press slices down to absorb egg mixture. Spoon any egg mixture that bread has not absorbed over bread slices.

3. In cup, mix cinnamon with remaining 1 tablespoon sugar; sprinkle over top of bread pudding and dot with 2 tablespoons butter. Cover and refrigerate at least 30 minutes or overnight.

◆ *Bread Pudding with Warm Banana-Maple Sauce and Orange-Cranberry Fizz*

4. Preheat oven to 325°F. Remove cover from bread pudding and bake 45 minutes, or until knife inserted in center comes out clean.

5. Meanwhile, prepare banana sauce: In nonstick 12-inch skillet, melt remaining 2 tablespoons butter over medium-high heat. Add banana slices and cook about 3 minutes, until lightly browned. Pour maple syrup over bananas; heat to boiling. Boil 2 to 3 minutes, until mixture thickens slightly. Serve warm sauce in bowl with bread pudding. Makes 12 main-dish servings.

Each serving with sauce: About 365 calories, 11 g protein, 52 g carbohydrate, 13 g total fat (4 g saturated), 205 mg cholesterol, 410 mg sodium.

ORANGE-CRANBERRY FIZZ

PREP: 10 MINUTES

> 1 quart cranberry-raspberry juice blend, chilled
> 2 cups cranberry or plain ginger ale, chilled
> 2 cups orange juice
> 2 cups lemon-lime seltzer, chilled
> orange and lime slices, and cranberries for garnish
>   (optional)

In large pitcher (about 3 quarts), mix cranberry-raspberry juice, ginger ale, and orange juice. Refrigerate until ready to serve. Just before serving, stir in seltzer. Garnish with orange and lime slices, and cranberries, if you like. Makes about 10 cups or 10 servings.

Each serving: About 95 calories, 0 g protein, 24 g carbohydrate, 0 g total fat (0 g saturated), 0 mg cholesterol, 20 mg sodium.

◆ *Puffy Cheddar Grits and*
Oven-Baked Pepper Bacon

PUFFY CHEDDAR GRITS

PREP: 20 MINUTES
BAKE: 45 MINUTES

2 tablespoons butter or margarine
1 teaspoon salt
3½ cups milk
2 cups water
1¼ cups quick-cooking grits
1 package (8 ounces) shredded Cheddar cheese
(2 cups)
1 teaspoon hot pepper sauce
¼ teaspoon pepper
5 large eggs

1. Preheat oven to 325°F. In 3-quart saucepan, combine butter, salt, 1 ½ cups milk, and water and heat to boiling over medium-high heat. Gradually stir in grits, beating constantly with wire whisk to prevent lumps. Reduce heat; cover and cook, stirring occasionally, 5 minutes. (Grits will be very stiff.) Remove saucepan from heat; blend in cheese.

2. In large bowl, with wire whisk or fork, mix hot pepper sauce, pepper, eggs, and remaining 2 cups milk until blended. Gradually stir grits mixture into egg mixture.

3. Grease shallow 2½-quart casserole. Pour grits mixture into casserole. Bake, uncovered, 45 minutes, or until knife inserted in center comes out clean. Makes 12 main-dish servings.

Each serving: About 230 calories, 12 g protein, 17 g carbohydrate, 13 g total fat (7 g saturated), 118 mg cholesterol, 385 mg sodium.

OVEN-BAKED PEPPER BACON

PREP: 10 MINUTES
BAKE: 25 MINUTES

1 ½ pounds sliced lean bacon
2 ½ teaspoons coarsely ground black pepper

1. Preheat oven to 400°F. Arrange bacon slices in 2 jelly-roll or shallow roasting pans, overlapping the lean edge of each slice with the fat edge of the next.

2. Evenly sprinkle pepper over bacon slices. Place pans on 2 oven racks and bake 25 minutes, switching pans between upper and lower racks halfway through baking, or until bacon is golden brown and crisp. Transfer bacon to paper towels to drain; keep warm. Makes 12 accompaniment servings.

Each serving: About 90 calories, 5 g protein, 0 g carbohydrate, 8 g total fat (3 g saturated), 13 mg cholesterol, 255 mg sodium.

FESTIVE CHRISTMAS TREE ROLLS

PREP: 45 MINUTES PLUS RISING AND COOLING
BAKE: 20 TO 25 MINUTES

2 packages active dry yeast
¼ cup granulated sugar
1 ½ teaspoons ground cardamom
about 4 ¾ cups all-purpose flour
1 ½ plus 1/8 teaspoons salt
½ cup butter or margarine (1 stick)
1 cup plus 1 tablespoon water
2 large eggs
½ cup golden raisins
½ cup diced mixed candied fruit
¾ cup confectioners' sugar

1. In large bowl, combine yeast, granulated sugar, cardamom, 1 ½ cups flour, and 1 ½ teaspoons salt. In 1-quart saucepan, heat butter and 1 cup water over low heat until very warm (120° to 130°F). Butter does not need to melt completely.

2. With mixer at low speed, gradually beat liquid into dry ingredients just until blended. Increase speed to medium; beat 2 minutes, occasionally scraping bowl with rubber spatula. Beat in 1 egg, 1 egg yolk, and ½ cup flour to make a thick batter; continue beating 2 minutes, scraping bowl often. Reserve remaining egg white. With wooden spoon, stir in 2 ½ cups flour to make a soft dough.

3. Turn dough onto lightly floured surface and knead until smooth and elastic, about 10 minutes, working in more flour (about ¼ cup) if needed to keep dough from sticking to work surface. Shape dough into a ball; place in greased large bowl, turning dough to grease top. Cover; let rise in warm place (80° to 85°F) about 1 hour, until doubled.

4. Punch down dough. Knead in raisins and candied fruit. Cut dough into 25 equal pieces; let rest 15 minutes for easier shaping. Shape into balls.

5. To make Christmas tree, place 1 dough ball at top of lightly greased large cookie sheet. Make a second row by centering 2 dough balls directly under the first ball and placing balls ¼ inch apart to allow space for rising. Continue making rows by increasing each row by 1 ball and centering balls directly under previous row, until there are 6 rows in all. Leave space to allow for rising. Use last 4 balls to make trunk of tree. Cover and let rise about 40 minutes, until doubled.

6. Preheat oven to 375°F. In cup, with fork, beat reserved egg white with remaining 1/8 teaspoon salt. Brush rolls with egg white. Bake rolls 20 to 25 minutes, until golden and rolls sound hollow when lightly tapped. With wide spatula, transfer rolls to wire rack to cool, about 1 hour.

7. When cool, prepare glaze: In bowl, mix confectioners' sugar and remaining 1 tablespoon water. With spoon, drizzle glaze in zigzag pattern over tree. Makes 25 rolls.

Each roll: About 180 calories, 3 g protein, 32 g carbohydrate, 4 g total fat (1 g saturated), 17 mg cholesterol, 195 mg sodium.

CHOCOLATE-CHERRY COFFEE CAKE

PREP: 30 MINUTES PLUS COOLING
BAKE: 1 HOUR 10 MINUTES

½ cup semisweet chocolate mini pieces
1 tablespoon unsweetened cocoa
2 teaspoons ground cinnamon
1 ⅔ cups granulated sugar
¾ cup butter or margarine, softened
  (1 ½ sticks)
3 cups all-purpose flour
1 ½ teaspoons baking soda
1 ½ teaspoons baking powder
2 teaspoons vanilla extract
½ teaspoon salt
1 container (16 ounces) light sour cream
3 large eggs
⅔ cup dried cherries
confectioners' sugar for garnish (optional)

1. Preheat oven to 325°F. Grease and flour 10-inch Bundt pan. In small bowl, combine chocolate mini pieces, cocoa, cinnamon, and ⅓ cup granulated sugar; set aside.

2. In large bowl, with mixer at low speed, beat butter and remaining 1 ⅓ cups granulated sugar until blended. Increase speed to medium; beat 2 minutes, occasionally scraping bowl with rubber spatula.

3. Reduce speed to low. Add flour, baking soda, baking powder, vanilla extract, salt, sour cream, and eggs; beat until well mixed. Increase speed to medium; beat 2 minutes, scraping bowl. Stir in dried cherries.

4. Spread one-third of batter in Bundt pan; sprinkle with half the chocolate mixture. Top with half the remaining batter; sprinkle with remaining chocolate mixture. Spread remaining batter on top.

5. Bake coffee cake 1 hour 10 minutes, or until toothpick inserted in center of cake comes out clean. Cool cake in pan on wire rack 10 minutes. Invert cake onto wire rack to cool completely.

6. Sift confectioners' sugar over cake before serving, if you like. Makes 16 servings.

Each serving: About 335 calories, 5 g protein, 49 g carbohydrate, 13 g total fat (2 g saturated), 49 mg cholesterol, 370 mg sodium.

HOLIDAY FRUIT COMPOTE

PREP: 30 MINUTES PLUS CHILLING
COOK: 15 MINUTES

3 medium oranges
1 ¼ cups sugar
2 tablespoons lemon juice
1 cinnamon stick (3 inches)
2 cups water
1 medium red eating apple, unpeeled, cored, and
  cut into thin wedges
1 medium pear, unpeeled, cored, and cut into
  thin wedges
3 medium pink or red grapefruits

1. From 1 orange, remove 1-inch-wide continuous strip of peel. In 2-quart saucepan, combine orange peel, sugar, lemon juice, cinnamon stick, and water and heat to boiling over medium-high heat. Reduce heat; cover and simmer 15 minutes, or until syrup thickens slightly. Remove pan from heat. Add apple and pear wedges; let stand 30 minutes at room temperature to soften fruit slightly.

2. Meanwhile, from 1 remaining orange, cut peel into thin strips; wrap with plastic wrap and refrigerate for garnish later. Cut peel from grapefruits and remaining orange and discard. Holding oranges and grapefruits over medium bowl to catch juice, cut sections from between membranes and add to bowl.

3. Add apple mixture to orange and grapefruit sections; cover and refrigerate until well chilled, at least 4 hours or overnight. Garnish with orange-peel strips to serve. Makes 12 servings.

Each serving: About 135 calories, 1 g protein, 35 g carbohydrate, 0 g total fat (0 g saturated), 0 mg cholesterol, 1 mg sodium.

◆ *Chocolate-Cherry Coffee Cake*
   and Holiday Fruit Compote

Breads

REFRIGERATOR POTATO ROLLS

PREP: I HOURS 30 MINUTES PLUS RISING AND OVERNIGHT TO CHILL

BAKE: 25 MINUTES

*3 medium all-purpose potatoes (1 pound), peeled
  and cut into 1-inch pieces*
2 tablespoons sugar
1 tablespoon salt
2 packages quick-rise yeast
about 9 ¾ cups all-purpose flour
4 tablespoons butter or margarine
2 large eggs

1. In 2-quart saucepan, heat potatoes and *4 cups water* to boiling over high heat. Reduce heat; cover and simmer 15 minutes, or until potatoes are fork-tender. Drain potatoes, reserving 2 cups potato cooking water. Return potatoes to saucepan. With potato masher, mash potatoes until smooth; set aside.

2. In large bowl, combine sugar, salt, yeast, and 3 cups flour. In 1-quart saucepan, combine butter and reserved potato water and heat water over low heat until very warm (120° to 130°F). Butter does not need to melt completely.

3. With mixer at low speed, gradually beat warm liquid into dry ingredients just until blended. Increase speed to medium; beat 2 minutes, occasionally scraping bowl with rubber spatula. Gradually beat in 1 egg, 1 egg yolk, and 1 cup flour to make a thick batter; continue beating 2 minutes, scraping bowl often. Refrigerate remaining egg white to brush on rolls later. With wooden spoon, stir in mashed potatoes, then 5 cups flour, 1 cup at a time, to make a soft dough. (You may want to transfer mixture to a larger bowl for easier mixing.)

4. Turn dough onto well-floured surface and knead until smooth and elastic, about 10 minutes, working in more flour (about ¾ cup) while kneading. Cut dough into 24 equal pieces; cover and let rest 15 minutes. Grease large roasting pan (17" by 11½").

5. Shape dough into balls and place in roasting pan. Cover pan with plastic wrap and refrigerate overnight. (You can bake rolls the same day. After shaping into balls, cover and let rise in warm place about 40 minutes, until doubled, then bake as directed in step 7.)

6. When ready to bake, remove plastic wrap; cover with towel and let rise in warm place (80° to 85°F) about 30 minutes, until doubled.

7. Preheat oven to 400°F. With fork, beat reserved egg white. Brush rolls with egg white. Bake rolls 25 to 30 minutes, until golden and rolls sound hollow when lightly tapped. Cool slightly to serve warm. Or, remove rolls from pan and cool on wire rack to serve later. Reheat if desired. Pull rolls apart to serve. Makes 2 dozen rolls.

Each roll: About 225 calories, 6 g protein, 43 g carbohydrate, 3 g total fat (1 g saturated), 18 mg cholesterol, 300 mg sodium.

◆ *Refrigerator Potato Rolls and New England Brown Bread*

NEW ENGLAND BROWN BREAD

PREP: 15 MINUTES PLUS COOLING
BAKE: 55 TO 60 MINUTES

1 cup all-purpose flour
1 cup whole-wheat flour
¾ cup dark seedless raisins
¼ cup sugar
1 ¼ teaspoons baking soda
½ teaspoon salt
1 ¼ cups buttermilk or plain low-fat yogurt
¾ cup light molasses
1 large egg

1. Preheat oven to 350°F. Grease 9" by 5" metal loaf pan. In large bowl, combine flours, raisins, sugar, baking soda, and salt. Stir in buttermilk, molasses, and egg until batter is just mixed (batter will be very wet).

2. Pour batter into loaf pan. Bake bread 55 to 60 minutes, until toothpick inserted in center of bread comes out clean.

3. With spatula, loosen bread from sides of pan. Remove bread from pan; cool slightly on wire rack to serve warm. Or, cool completely to serve later. Makes 1 loaf, 12 servings.

Each serving: About 180 calories, 4 g protein, 41 g carbohydrate, 1 g total fat (0 g saturated), 19 mg cholesterol, 255 mg sodium.

Desserts

TIRAMISU CAKE

PREP: 30 MINUTES PLUS OVERNIGHT TO CHILL
BAKE: 10 TO 12 MINUTES

CAKE

¾ cup sugar
4 large eggs
1 cup all-purpose flour

COFFEE SYRUP

1 cup (8 ounces) hot espresso or very strong
* brewed coffee*
2 tablespoons sugar
3 tablespoons brandy

FILLING

1 container (16 to 17 ½ ounces) mascarpone cheese
½ cup milk
½ cup sugar
¾ cup heavy or whipping cream
4 squares (4 ounces) semisweet chocolate, grated
3 tablespoons unsweetened cocoa powder for dusting
Chocolate Curls for garnish (see below), optional

1. Prepare cake: Preheat oven to 400°F. Grease three 8-inch round cake pans; line bottoms with waxed paper; grease paper. Dust pans with flour.
2. In large bowl, with mixer at low speed, beat sugar with eggs until blended. Increase speed to high; beat 5 to 10 minutes, until mixture is pale, thick, and creamy, and batter forms a thick ribbon when beaters are lifted. With rubber spatula, gently fold in flour until mixture is well-combined.
3. Pour batter into pans. Bake 8 to 10 minutes, until toothpick inserted in center of cake comes out clean.

Cool in pans 1 minute; then invert onto wire rack to cool completely .
4. Prepare coffee syrup: In small bowl, stir together espresso, 2 tablespoons sugar, and brandy; let cool.
5. Prepare filling: In large bowl, with mixer at high speed, beat mascarpone, milk, and ½ cup sugar 3 minutes, or until very light and fluffy.
6. In small bowl, with same beaters, beat cream to soft peaks. With rubber spatula, gently fold whipped cream into mascarpone mixture.
7. Place 1 cake round, smooth side down, on cake plate. With pastry brush, brush one-third of coffee syrup over cake. Spread half the cheese filling, followed by half the grated chocolate. Continue layering the ingredients, ending with the third cake layer brushed with syrup. Cover and refrigerate overnight.
8. To serve, dust cake with cocoa and decorate with chocolate curls, if desired. Makes 16 servings.

Each serving without chocolate curls: About 339 calories, 5 g protein, 31 g carbohydrate, 22 g total fat (14 g saturated) 94 mg cholesterol, 40 mg sodium.

CHOCOLATE CURLS: In 1-quart saucepan, heat 3 ounces (½ cup) semisweet chocolate pieces with 1 tablespoon vegetable shortening over low heat, stirring frequently, until melted and smooth. Pour chocolate mixture into foil-lined or disposable 5 ¾" by 3 ¼" loaf pan. Refrigerate about 2 hours, until chocolate is set. Remove chocolate from pan. Using a vegetable peeler, draw blade across surface of chocolate to make large curls. If chocolate appears too brittle to curl, let stand at room temperature 30 minutes to soften slightly. To avoid breaking curls, use a toothpick to lift and transfer to cake.

◆ *Tiramisu Cake*

AUSTRIAN DRUM TORTE

PREP: 2 HOURS 30 MINUTES PLUS CHILLING
AND COOLING

BAKE: 10 TO 12 MINUTES PER BATCH

CHOCOLATE GANACHE

*1 package (8 ounces) semisweet chocolate squares,
  very finely chopped*
1 bar (3 ounces) milk chocolate, very finely chopped
1 cup heavy or whipping cream
4 tablespoons butter or margarine, cut up

SPONGE CAKE

12 large eggs, separated
1 cup sugar
2 teaspoons vanilla extract
1 1/3 cups cake flour (not self-rising)
3 tablespoons butter or margarine, melted

CARAMEL

1/3 cup sugar
1 tablespoon butter or margarine
1 teaspoon fresh lemon juice
2 tablespoons water
1 square (1 ounce) semisweet chocolate, melted

1. Prepare chocolate ganache: In medium bowl (preferably metal), combine semisweet and milk chocolates; set aside. In 2-quart saucepan, heat cream to boiling over medium-high heat. Pour over chocolate in bowl; let stand 1 minute. With rubber spatula, stir until mixture is smooth. Stir in butter until melted and smooth.

2. Place *2 inches cold water* and about *2 cups ice cubes* in very large bowl to make an ice bath. Set bowl with ganache in ice bath and chill, stirring ganache occasionally with rubber spatula, about 20 minutes, until mixture thickens and is an easy spreading consistency. (Or, chill uncovered in refrigerator at least 4 hours or

overnight. Let come to room temperature; stir with spoon until an easy spreading consistency.)

3. Prepare sponge cake: Preheat oven to 400°F. Grease bottoms of two 9-inch round metal cake pans. Line each pan with a 9-inch reusable nonstick bakeware liner, or kitchen parchment, or waxed paper; grease parchment or waxed paper. (If using parchment or waxed paper, you will need to cut a total of seven 9-inch rounds. Liners are reusable and just need to be wiped clean.)

4. In small bowl, with mixer at high speed, beat egg yolks with 1/2 cup sugar about 10 minutes, until thick and lemon-colored. Beat in vanilla; set aside.

5. In large bowl, with clean beaters and with mixer at high speed, beat egg whites until soft peaks form. Beating at high speed, gradually sprinkle in remaining 1/2 cup sugar, 2 tablespoons at a time, beating well after each addition until sugar dissolves and whites stand in stiff peaks.

6. Transfer yolk mixture to very large bowl. Gradually sift in and fold flour into yolk mixture, then fold in melted butter until blended.

7. With spatula, fold beaten egg-white mixture into yolk mixture, one-third at a time, just until blended.

8. Spoon about 1 cup batter into each prepared pan. With metal spatula (preferably offset), gently spread batter to even thickness. Bake cake layers about 10 minutes, until lightly golden and cake springs back when gently touched with finger. Loosen edge of each layer with metal spatula; invert onto wire rack to cool completely. (If using liners, wipe clean before reusing. If using parchment or waxed paper, remove from layers after layers are cooled.)

9. When pans are cool, repeat with remaining batter to make 7 layers in all. Stack cooled cake layers between sheets of waxed paper.

10. Prepare caramel: In 1-quart saucepan, combine sugar, butter, lemon juice, and water and heat to boiling over high heat. Continue cooking, without stirring, about 4 minutes, until caramel is golden brown.

◆ *Austrian Drum Torte*

(A) Carefully spread warm homemade caramel evenly over 1 cake layer with metal spatula. (B) After caramel cools and layer is cut into 16 wedges, dip rounded edge of each wedge into melted semisweet chocolate. (C) Arrange wedges on assembled cake, resting each on a ganache dollop at a 45-degree angle.

11. Carefully pour hot caramel over top of 1 cake layer; spread evenly with metal spatula (A). Cool caramel 2 minutes to set. With greased chef's knife, cut layer in 16 wedges (do not let caramel cool too long; it will crack when it is cut). Dip rounded outside edge of each wedge into melted chocolate (B); place on waxed paper-lined cookie sheet to set.

12. To assemble cake: Spread ⅓ cup chocolate ganache on 1 cake layer. Top with second layer and spread with ⅓ cup ganache. Repeat 4 more times. Spoon remaining ganache into 16 dollops evenly spaced around edge of top layer. If serving within 2 hours, place 1 caramel-coated wedge, set at an angle, on top of each dollop (C). If not serving right away, refrigerate cake, but do not place wedges on top; the caramel will get soft in refrigerator.

13. To serve, remove cake from refrigerator at least 1 hour before serving, top with caramel wedges. Makes 16 servings.

Each serving: About 360 calories, 7 g protein, 39 g carbohydrate, 20 g total fat (7 g saturated), 180 mg cholesterol, 145 mg sodium.

CREAM-PUFF WREATH

PREP: 50 MINUTES PLUS CHILLING
BAKE: 55 MINUTES

PASTRY CREAM

3 large egg yolks
⅓ cup granulated sugar
3 tablespoons cornstarch
2 cups milk
2 teaspoons vanilla extract

WREATH

6 tablespoons butter or margarine, cut up
1 cup water
1 cup all-purpose flour
4 large eggs

ALMOND PRALINE

⅓ cup granulated sugar
¼ cup water
½ cup sliced natural almonds, toasted
1 cup heavy or whipping cream
1 tablespoon confectioners' sugar plus additional
  for garnish

1. Prepare pastry cream: In medium bowl, with wire whisk, beat egg yolks, granulated sugar, and cornstarch until blended. In 3-quart saucepan, heat milk to simmering over medium-high heat. While constantly beating with wire whisk, gradually pour about half of simmering milk into yolk mixture. Return yolk mixture to saucepan and cook over low heat, whisking constantly, until mixture thickens and begins to bubble around edge of pan (mixture will not appear to boil vigorously); simmer 1 minute. Remove saucepan from heat; stir in vanilla. Transfer mixture to bowl. Cover surface directly with plastic wrap to prevent skin from forming and refrigerate at least 2 hours, until cold.

2. Meanwhile prepare wreath: Preheat oven to 425°F. Grease and flour large cookie sheet. Using 8-inch cake pan or plate as guide, trace circle in flour on cookie sheet with finger. Cut 1-inch opening from 1 corner of large zip-tight plastic bag.

3. In 2-quart saucepan, heat butter with water over high heat until butter melts and mixture boils. Reduce heat; add flour all at once and stir vigorously with wooden spoon until mixture forms ball and leaves side of saucepan. Remove from heat. Add eggs, 1 at a time, beating well with wooden spoon after each addition, until batter is smooth and satiny.

4. Spoon dough into plastic bag; squeeze down to corner with opening. Using traced circle as guide, pipe dough in 1-inch-thick ring just inside circle on cookie sheet. Pipe another 1-inch-thick ring outside of first, making sure both are touching. With remaining dough, pipe a final ring on top along center seam of first 2 rings. With moistened finger, gently smooth dough rings where ends meet.

5. Bake wreath 20 minutes. Turn oven control to 375°F and bake 25 minutes longer, or until golden. Remove wreath from oven; poke side in several places with toothpick and bake 10 minutes longer. Transfer wreath to wire rack and cool completely.

6. While wreath is cooling, prepare almond praline: Lightly grease cookie sheet. In 1-quart saucepan, heat granulated sugar and water to boiling over high heat, swirling pan occasionally to help dissolve sugar. Boil mixture, without stirring, 5 to 7 minutes, until golden. Remove pan from heat and stir in ⅓ cup almonds; reserve remaining almonds for garnish. Stir mixture over low heat just until it liquefies. Immediately pour praline mixture onto cookie sheet; spread with back of spoon to ½-inch thickness. Let praline cool on cookie sheet on wire rack 10 minutes, or until firm.

7. Break praline into small pieces. In food processor with knife blade attached, process praline until ground into a fine powder.

◆ *Cream Puff Wreath*

8. *Assemble wreath:* With long serrated knife, slice wreath horizontally in half. If you like, pull out some of the moist interior of wreath and discard. In small bowl, with mixer at medium speed, beat cream and 1 tablespoon confectioners' sugar until stiff peaks form. Gently fold praline into chilled pastry cream; spoon into bottom of wreath. Top with whipped cream. Replace top of wreath. Refrigerate dessert if not serving right away.

9. To serve, sprinkle with confectioners' sugar; garnish with reserved almonds. Makes 12 servings.

Each serving: About 295 calories, 7 g protein, 25 g carbohydrate, 19 g total fat (8 g saturated), 157 mg cholesterol, 125 mg sodium.

◆ *Strawberry Dacquoise and*
Oven-Steamed Figgy Pudding

STRAWBERRY DACQUOISE

PREP: 1 HOUR PLUS CHILLING
BAKE: 1 HOUR PLUS 1 HOUR 15 MINUTES TO DRY
IN OVEN

1 cup pecans, toasted
2 tablespoons cornstarch
1½ cups plus 3 tablespoons confectioners' sugar
6 large egg whites
½ teaspoon cream of tartar
1 package (10 ounces) frozen quick-thaw
  strawberries in light syrup, thawed
1 envelope unflavored gelatin
2 cups heavy or whipping cream
1 pint strawberries

1. In food processor with knife blade attached, or in blender at medium speed, process pecans, cornstarch, and ¾ cup confectioners' sugar until pecans are finely ground.

2. Line large cookie sheet with foil. With toothpick, outline three 13" by 4" rectangles on foil. Spray with nonstick cooking spray. Preheat oven to 275°F.

3. In large bowl, with mixer at high speed, beat egg whites and cream of tartar to soft peaks. Sprinkle in ¾ cup confectioners' sugar, 2 tablespoons at a time, beating well after each addition until sugar completely dissolves and whites stand in stiff, glossy peaks.

4. With rubber spatula, carefully fold ground pecan mixture into egg-white mixture. With metal spatula, spread one-third of meringue inside each rectangle on cookie sheet. Bake meringues 1 hour. Turn oven off; leave meringues in oven 1 hour 15 minutes to dry.

5. Cool meringues on cookie sheet on wire rack 10 minutes. Peel foil from meringues and cool completely. Store in airtight container at room temperature (to prevent sogginess) until ready to assemble.

6. In 2-quart saucepan, mash quick-thaw strawberries with their syrup. Sprinkle gelatin evenly over crushed strawberries; let stand 5 minutes to soften gelatin. Place saucepan over medium heat and cook strawberry mixture, stirring constantly, 2 to 3 minutes, until gelatin dissolves completely. Pour mixture into small bowl; chill over bowl of ice, stirring occasionally, about 15 minutes, until mixture thickens slightly to the consistency of egg whites.

7. In small bowl, with mixer at medium speed, beat heavy or whipping cream and remaining 3 tablespoons confectioners' sugar until stiff peaks form. Gently fold in thickened strawberry mixture.

8. On serving plate, place 1 meringue layer; spread with one-third of strawberry-cream filling. Repeat with remaining meringue layers and strawberry filling, ending with strawberry filling. Cover dacquoise with plastic wrap and refrigerate 4 hours to soften meringue layers for easier cutting.

9. To serve, hull strawberries. Cut one-third of strawberries in half; slice remaining berries. Arrange halved and sliced berries on top of dacquoise. Dust with confectioners' sugar, if you like. Makes 12 servings.

Each serving: About 305 calories, 4 g protein, 28 g carbohydrate, 21 g total fat (10 g saturated), 54 mg cholesterol, 45 mg sodium.

OVEN-STEAMED FIGGY PUDDING

PREP: 45 MINUTES
BAKE: 2 HOURS

2 packages (8 ounces each) dried Calimyrna figs
1 ¾ cups milk
1 ½ cups all-purpose flour
1 cup sugar
2 ½ teaspoons baking powder
1 teaspoon ground nutmeg
1 teaspoon ground cinnamon
1 teaspoon salt
3 large eggs
½ cup butter or margarine (1 stick), melted and
* cooled slightly*
1 ½ cups fresh bread crumbs (from 3 to 4 slices
* white bread)*
2 teaspoons grated orange peel
1 teaspoon grated lemon peel
marzipan fruit and greens for garnish
Brandied Hard Sauce (see below)

1. Preheat oven to 350°F. Grease 2½-quart metal steamed-pudding mold or fluted tube pan.
2. With kitchen shears, cut stems from figs; cut figs into small pieces. In 2-quart saucepan, combine figs and milk; cover and cook over medium-low heat, stirring occasionally; 10 to 15 minutes (mixture may look curdled). Be careful not to let mixture boil.
3. Meanwhile, in medium bowl, mix, flour, sugar, baking powder, nutmeg, cinnamon, and salt.

4. In large bowl, with mixer at high speed, beat eggs 1 minute. Reduce speed to low; add butter, bread crumbs, orange peel, lemon peel, and fig mixture. Gradually add flour mixture; beat just until blended.
5. Spoon fig mixture into mold, smoothing top. Cover with sheet of greased foil, greased-side down. (If your mold has a lid, grease the inside and do not use foil.) Place the mold in a deep roasting pan and place on oven rack. Pour hot tap *water* into roasting pan to come 2 inches up side of mold.
6. Bake pudding 2 hours or until firm and it pulls away from side of mold. Transfer pudding to wire rack; remove foil and cool 10 minutes. Invert onto serving plate; remove mold. Garnish with marzipan fruit and greens. Serve warm with brandied Hard Sauce, if desired. Makes 12 servings.

Each serving without hard sauce: About 350 calories, 6 g protein, 59g carbohydrate, 11 g total fat (3g saturated), 58 mg cholesterol, 430 mg sodium.

BRANDIED HARD SAUCE: In small bowl, with mixer at medium speed, beat 1½ cups confectioners' sugar, ½ cup butter or margarine (1 stick) softened, 2 tablespoons brandy, and ½ teaspoon vanilla extract until creamy. Refrigerate if not serving right away. Makes about 1 cup.

Each tablespoon: About 105 calories, 0 g protein, 11 g carbohydrate, 6 g total fat (1 g saturated), 0 mg cholesterol, 75 mg sodium.

◆ *A delicious classic, Figgy Pudding was once an all-day activity of mixing ingredients,*
then steaming on the stovetop. Here, the ingredient list is lightened—we used butter
instead of suet—and the cooking simplified—oven steaming is easy and foolproof.
All the traditional flavor remains, but the preparation is streamlined for the nineties.

Brandied Bûche de Noël

PREP: 1 HOUR 30 MINUTES PLUS COOLING AND CHILLING
BAKE: 10 MINUTES

CAKE

⅓ cup all-purpose flour
¼ cup unsweetened cocoa
1 teaspoon ground cinnamon
1 teaspoon ground ginger
pinch ground cloves
pinch salt
5 large eggs, separated
¼ teaspoon cream of tartar
½ cup granulated sugar
2 tablespoons butter or margarine, melted and cooled slightly
confectioners' sugar
nontoxic greens
Meringue Mushrooms (see below)

BRANDIED BUTTER CREAM

1 cup granulated sugar
½ cup all-purpose flour
1 cup milk
1 square (1 ounce) unsweetened chocolate
1 square (1 ounce) semisweet chocolate
1 cup (2 sticks) butter or margarine, softened
2 tablespoons brandy
1 teaspoon vanilla extract

1. **Prepare cake roll:** Preheat oven to 375°F. Grease 15½" by 10½" jelly-roll pan; line with waxed paper. Grease paper and dust with flour.

2. On sheet of waxed paper, combine flour, cocoa, cinnamon, ginger, cloves, and salt.

3. In small bowl, with mixer at high speed, beat egg whites and cream of tartar until soft peaks form. Beating at high speed, gradually sprinkle in ¼ cup granulated sugar, beating until sugar dissolves and whites stand in stiff peaks.

4. In large bowl, using same beaters and with mixer at high speed, beat egg yolks and remaining ¼ cup granulated sugar until very thick and lemon-colored.

5. With rubber spatula or wire whisk, gently fold beaten egg whites into beaten egg yolks, one-third at a time; then gently fold flour mixture into egg mixture, one-third at a time. Fold in melted butter, mixing just until combined.

6. With metal spatula, spread batter evenly in prepared pan. Bake 10 minutes, or until top of cake springs back when lightly touched with finger.

7. Sprinkle clean cloth towel with confectioners' sugar. When cake is done, immediately invert hot cake onto towel. Peel off waxed paper and discard. Starting from a long side, roll cake with towel jelly-roll fashion. Cool cake roll, seam side down, on wire rack about 1 hour, until completely cool.

8. **Meanwhile, prepare brandied butter cream:** In 2-quart saucepan, combine granulated sugar and flour. With wire whisk, mix in milk until smooth. Cook over medium-high heat, stirring often, until mixture thickens and boils. Reduce heat and cook, stirring constantly, 2 minutes. Cool completely.

9. Meanwhile, in small saucepan, melt chocolates over low heat; cool slightly.

10. In large bowl, with mixer at medium speed, beat butter until creamy. Gradually beat in cooled flour mixture. When mixture is smooth, beat in brandy and vanilla extract until blended. Spoon half of white butter cream into small bowl; stir melted chocolate into butter cream remaining in large bowl.

11. **Assemble cake:** Gently unroll cooled cake. With metal spatula, spread white brandied butter cream almost to edges. Starting from a long side, roll cake without towel. With sharp knife, cut 1½-inch-thick diagonal slice off each end of roll; set aside. Place rolled cake, seam side down, on long platter. Spread some chocolate brandied butter cream over roll. Place

◆ *Brandied Bûche de Noël*

1 end piece on side of roll to resemble branch. Place remaining end piece on top of roll to resemble another branch. Spread remaining frosting over roll and branches, leaving cut side of branches unfrosted. With metal spatula, spread frosting to resemble bark of tree. Refrigerate cake at least 2 hours before serving. Garnish platter with greens and meringue mushrooms. Makes 14 servings

Each serving: About 310 calories, 4 g protein, 33 g carbohydrate, 19 g total fat (4 g saturated), 78 mg cholesterol, 240 mg sodium.

MERINGUE MUSHROOMS

PREP: 20 MINUTES PLUS COOLING
COOK: 2 HOURS

> *2 large egg whites*
> *⅛ teaspoon cream of tartar*
> *⅓ cup sugar*
> *unsweetened cocoa (optional)*
> *1 square (1 ounce) semisweet chocolate, melted*

1. Line large cookie sheet with foil.
2. In small bowl, with mixer at high speed, beat egg whites and cream of tartar until soft peaks form; grad-

ually beat in sugar, 2 tablespoons at a time, beating well after each addition, until sugar completely dissolves and whites stand in stiff, glossy peaks.
3. Preheat oven to 200°F. Spoon meringue into large decorating bag with large writing tip. Pipe meringue onto cookie sheet in 15 mounds, each about 1½ inches in diameter, to resemble mushroom caps. If you like, place some cocoa in small, fine-meshed strainer; use to dust meringue mushroom caps. Pipe remaining meringue onto cookie sheet in 15 upright 1¼-inch lengths to resemble mushroom stems.
4. Bake meringues 1½ hours. Turn oven off; let meringues stand in oven 30 minutes longer to dry. Cool completely on cookie sheet on wire rack.
5. With tip of paring knife, cut a small hole in center of underside of 1 mushroom cap. Dip pointed end of mushroom stem in melted chocolate; attach stem to cap by inserting chocolate-dipped end into hole in underside of mushroom cap. Repeat with remaining caps and stems. Let chocolate dry, about 1 hour.
6. Store mushrooms in tightly covered container up to one week. Makes 15 mushrooms.

Each mushroom: About 30 calories, 1 g protein, 6 g carbohydrate, 0 g total fat, 0 mg cholesterol, 10 mg sodium.

CRANBERRY-ALMOND TART

PREP: 40 MINUTES PLUS COOLING
BAKE: 1 HOUR

¼ teaspoon salt
1 cup plus 3 tablespoons all-purpose flour
8 tablespoons butter or margarine (1 stick)
2 to 3 tablespoons cold water plus ⅓ cup water
½ cup almond paste (about 5 ounces)
1 ¼ cups sugar
2 large eggs
½ teaspoon grated orange peel
1 bag (12-ounces) cranberries (3 cups)
lemon-peel strips for garnish

1. In medium bowl, mix salt and 1 cup flour. With pastry blender or 2 knives used scissor-fashion, cut in 4 tablespoons cold butter until mixture resembles coarse crumbs. Add 2 to 3 tablespoons cold water, 1 tablespoon at a time, mixing lightly with fork after each addition until dough is just moist enough to hold together. Shape dough into a disk; wrap with plastic wrap and freeze until firm enough to roll, about 15 minutes.

2. Meanwhile, in food processor with knife blade attached, blend almond paste, ½ cup sugar, and remaining 4 tablespoons softened butter until smooth. Add eggs and remaining 3 tablespoons flour; blend until well combined.

◆ *Cranberry-Almond Tart*

3. Preheat oven to 425°F. On lightly floured surface, with floured rolling pin, roll dough into 12-inch round. Press dough onto bottom and up side of 10" by 1" round tart pan with removable bottom. Fold overhang in and press against side of tart pan to form a thicker edge. With fork, prick dough all over to prevent puffing and shrinking during baking. Freeze 10 minutes, or until dough is firm.

4. Line tart shell with foil and fill with pie weights, dried beans, or uncooked rice. Bake tart shell 15 minutes, remove foil with weights and bake 10 minutes longer, or until golden. (If crust puffs up during baking, gently press it to tart pan with back of spoon.) Turn oven control to 350°F.

5. Fill hot tart shell with almond filling. Bake 20 to 25 minutes longer, until almond filling is slightly puffed and golden. Cool in pan on wire rack.

6. While tart shell is baking, in 2-quart saucepan, combine orange peel, 1 cup cranberries, remaining ¾ cup sugar, and ⅓ cup water and heat to boiling over high heat. Reduce heat to medium-low; simmer 5 minutes, or until mixture thickens slightly and cranberries pop. Stir in remaining 2 cups cranberries. Set aside until cool.

7. Remove almond-filled shell from pan; place on cake plate. Spoon cranberry topping over almond filling. Garnish with lemon-peel strips. Makes 10 servings.

Each serving: About 340 calories, 5 g protein, 48 g carbohydrate, 15 g total fat (2 g saturated), 43 mg cholesterol, 190 mg sodium.

◆ ***If you're pressed for time, make tart dough in a food processor. Using the knife blade, process flour, salt, shortening, and butter for 1 to 2 seconds. When mixture resembles fine crumbs, add an amount of ice water smaller than that called for in the recipe and process 1 to 2 seconds more, until dough begins to leave sides of bowl. Remove dough from bowl and shape into a ball.***

PRALINE-ICED BROWNIES

PREP: 20 MINUTES PLUS COOLING
BAKE: 35 MINUTES

BROWNIES

1 cup butter or margarine (2 sticks)
4 squares (4 ounces) unsweetened chocolate
4 squares (4 ounces) semisweet chocolate
2 ¼ cups granulated sugar
6 large eggs
2 teaspoons vanilla extract
½ teaspoon salt
1 ¼ cups all-purpose flour

PRALINE TOPPING

5 tablespoons butter or margarine
⅓ cup packed light brown sugar
3 tablespoons bourbon or 1 tablespoon
    vanilla extract
2 tablespoons water
2 cups confectioners' sugar
½ cup pecans, toasted and coarsely chopped

1. Preheat oven to 350°F. Line 13" by 9" metal baking pan with foil; grease foil.

2. In 3-quart saucepan, melt butter and chocolates over low heat, stirring frequently. Remove saucepan from heat. With wire whisk, beat in granulated sugar, then eggs, until well blended. Stir in vanilla, salt, then flour until blended. Spread batter evenly in pan.

3. Bake 35 minutes (toothpick inserted in brownies will not come out clean). Cool in pan on wire rack. If not using within 1 day, cover cooled brownies with foil and refrigerate or freeze for longer storage.

4. Prepare praline topping: In 2-quart saucepan, heat butter with brown sugar over medium-low heat, about 5 minutes, until mixture melts and bubbles. Remove saucepan from heat. With wire whisk, beat in

◆ *Praline-Iced Brownies and*
Ambrosia Layer Cake

bourbon or vanilla extract and water, then beat in confectioners' sugar until mixture is smooth.

5. With metal spatula, spread topping over room-temperature brownies; sprinkle with pecans. Cut brownies lengthwise into 8 strips, then cut each strip crosswise into 8 pieces. Makes 64 brownies.

Each iced brownie: About 120 calories, 1 g protein, 16 g carbohydrate, 6 g total fat (1 g saturated), 20 mg cholesterol, 75 mg sodium.

AMBROSIA LAYER CAKE

PREP: 1 HOUR 30 MINUTES PLUS COOLING
BAKE: 35 TO 40 MINUTES

ORANGE FILLING

4 large oranges
1 lemon
1 cup sugar
3 tablespoons cornstarch
½ cup butter or margarine (1 stick)
6 large egg yolks

CAKE

2 ½ cups cake flour (not self-rising)
1 ½ teaspoons baking powder
1 teaspoon baking soda
¼ teaspoon salt
1 ½ cups sugar
¾ cup butter or margarine (1 ½ sticks),
   softened
2 teaspoons vanilla extract
3 large eggs
1 cup buttermilk
1 cup flaked coconut
orange-peel curls for garnish

FLUFFY WHITE FROSTING

2 large egg whites
1 cup sugar
¼ cup water
2 teaspoons lemon juice
1 teaspoon light corn syrup
¼ teaspoon cream of tartar

1. Prepare orange filling: From oranges, grate 1 tablespoon peel and squeeze 1⅓ cups juice. From lemon, squeeze 1 tablespoon juice. In 3-quart saucepan, combine orange peel, orange juice, lemon juice, sugar, and cornstarch and stir until blended. Add butter and heat to boiling over medium heat; boil 1 minute.

2. In small bowl, beat yolks slightly. Into yolks, beat a small amount of orange mixture; pour egg mixture into orange mixture in saucepan. Reduce heat to low; cook, stirring constantly, 3 minutes, or until mixture is very thick. Pour into medium bowl; cover surface with plastic wrap to prevent skin from forming. Refrigerate until cold, about 2 hours.

3. Preheat oven to 350°F. Grease and flour 13" by 9" metal baking pan. In medium bowl, combine flour, baking powder, baking soda, and salt; set aside.

4. In large bowl, with mixer at low speed, beat sugar and butter just until blended. Increase speed to high; beat until light and fluffy, 5 minutes, scraping bowl often with rubber spatula. Reduce speed to low; add vanilla extract and eggs, 1 at a time, and continue beating until blended. Alternately add flour mixture and buttermilk, ending with flour, and beat, occasionally scraping bowl, until batter is well mixed.

5. Spread batter in pan. Bake 35 to 40 minutes, until toothpick inserted in center of cake comes out clean. Cool in pan on wire rack 10 minutes. Invert cake onto wire rack to cool completely.

6. Prepare fluffy white frosting: In top of double boiler, over simmering water, with handheld mixer at high speed, beat egg whites, sugar, water, lemon juice, corn syrup, and cream of tartar, about 7 to 10 minutes, until soft peaks form. Remove double-boiler top from bottom; continue beating at high speed, about 7 to 10 minutes, until stiff peaks form.

7. Assemble cake: With serrated knife, cut cake horizontally in half. To remove top cake layer, carefully place cookie sheet in between cut layers and lift off top layer. With metal spatula, spread cooled orange filling on bottom layer. Transfer top layer of cake onto bottom layer by gently sliding cake onto filling.

8. Frost top and side of cake with fluffy white frosting. Sprinkle with coconut. Garnish with orange-peel curls. Makes 20 servings.

Each serving: About 355 calories, 4 g protein, 52 g carbohydrate, 15 g total fat (4 g saturated), 96 mg cholesterol, 300 mg sodium.

Gifts
From the Kitchen

CANDIED CITRUS PEEL

PREP: 20 MINUTES PLUS COOLING AND DRYING
COOK: ABOUT 1 HOUR 30 MINUTES

3 large grapefruit or 5 navel oranges
3½ cups sugar
1½ cups water

1. Score peel of each fruit into quarters, cutting just through the rind and white pith. Pull peel from fruit (you should have about 14 ounces peel). Refrigerate fruit for another use. Cut grapefruit peel crosswise or orange peel lengthwise into strips about ¼ inch wide.
2. In 4-quart saucepan, combine peel and enough *water* to cover; heat to boiling over high heat. Boil 5 minutes; drain.
3. Repeat step 2, two more times, draining peel well and using fresh water each time (3 blanchings in all).
4. In 12-inch skillet, combine 2½ cups sugar with 1½ cups water; cook over high heat, stirring constantly, until sugar dissolves and mixture boils. Boil, stirring occasionally, 15 minutes. (If using a candy thermometer, temperature should read 230° to 235° F.)
5. Add drained peel to syrup in skillet and stir to coat evenly. Reduce heat and simmer, partially covered, 1 hour, or until peel has absorbed most of syrup, stirring occasionally. Remove cover and continue to simmer, stirring gently, until all syrup has been absorbed.
6. On sheet of waxed paper, place remaining 1 cup sugar. With tongs, lightly roll peel, a few pieces at a time, in sugar; place in single layer on wire racks. Let peel dry at least 12 hours or overnight. Dry longer if necessary; peels should be dry on the outside but still moist on the inside. Store at room temperature in air-tight container up to 1 month. Makes about 2 pounds.

Each ounce: About 95 calories, 0 g protein, 24 g carbohydrate, 0 g fat, 0 mg cholesterol, 0 mg sodium.

MARINATED OLIVES

PREP: 10 MINUTES PLUS CHILLING
CHILL: 5 MINUTES

¼ cup extra virgin olive oil
2 teaspoons fennel seeds, crushed
4 small bay leaves
2 pounds assorted Mediterranean olives (such as niçoise, picholine, Kalamata, and oil-cured)
6 strips (3" by 1" each) lemon peel
4 garlic cloves, crushed with side of chef's knife

1. In 1-quart saucepan, heat oil, fennel seeds, and bay leaves over medium heat until hot but not smoking. Remove saucepan from heat; let stand 10 minutes.
2. In large bowl, combine olive-oil mixture with olives, lemon peel, and garlic. Cover bowl and refrigerate olives at least 24 hours to allow flavors to develop, stirring occasionally. (Or, in large zip-tight plastic bag, combine all ingredients, turning to coat olives well. Seal bag, pressing out as much air as possible. Place on plate; refrigerate, turning bag occasionally.)
3. Spoon olives into jars for gift giving. Store in refrigerator up to 1 month. Makes about 6 cups.

Each ¼ cup: About 90 calories, 0 g protein, 3 g carbohydrate, 10 g total fat (1 g saturated), 0 mg cholesterol, 700 mg sodium.

◆ *Candied Citrus Peel*

ARRABBIATA SAUCE

PREP: 15 MINUTES
COOK: ABOUT 1 HOUR

½ cup extra virgin olive oil
6 garlic cloves, crushed with side of chef's knife
4 cans (35 ounces each) Italian plum tomatoes
1 tablespoon salt
1 to 1½ teaspoons crushed red pepper

1. In 8-quart Dutch oven, heat oil over medium heat until hot but not smoking. Add garlic and cook, stirring, 2 minutes; do not brown. Stir in tomatoes with their juice, salt, and red pepper; heat to boiling over high heat. Reduce heat; simmer, uncovered, 50 minutes, or until sauce thickens slightly, stirring occasionally and crushing tomatoes with side of spoon.

2. For smooth, traditional texture, press tomato mixture through food mill into large bowl. Or, leave sauce as is for a hearty, chunky texture. Cool sauce slightly. Spoon into jars. Store in refrigerator up to 1 week; or spoon into freezer-proof containers and freeze up to 2 months. Makes about 14 cups.

Each ¼ cup: About 30 calories, 1 g protein, 3 g carbohydrate, 2 g total fat (0 g saturated), 0 mg cholesterol, 230 mg sodium.

◆ *It's never too early to start collecting containers for all the goodies you'll give away at Christmas. Save jars with interesting shapes and in all sizes and spray their tops with gold or silver paint. Line unusual baskets with fabric printed with seasonal motifs, or thread bright-colored ribbons through open-weave baskets. Browse through summer flea markets for vintage cookie tins. Or use your new découpage skills (see page 36) to spiff up plain boxes and tins.*

ROSEMARY-FENNEL BREADSTICKS

PREP: 40 MINUTES
BAKE: 20 MINUTES PER BATCH

2 packages quick-rise yeast
2½ teaspoons salt
2 teaspoons fennel seeds, crushed
1 teaspoon dried rosemary, crumbled
½ teaspoon coarsely ground black pepper
about 4¾ cups all-purpose flour
1⅓ cups very warm water (120° to 130°F)
½ cup olive oil

1. In large bowl, combine yeast, salt, fennel seeds, rosemary, pepper, and 2 cups flour. With spoon, stir in warm water; beat vigorously with spoon 1 minute. Stir in oil. Gradually stir in 2¼ cups flour.

2. Turn dough onto floured surface and knead until smooth and elastic, about 8 minutes, working in more flour (about ½ cup) while kneading. Cover dough loosely with plastic wrap; let rest 10 minutes.

3. Preheat oven to 375°F. Grease 2 large cookie sheets. Divide dough in half. Keeping one-half of dough covered, cut other half into 32 pieces. Shape each piece into 12-inch-long rope. Place ropes, about 1 inch apart, on cookie sheets.

4. Place cookie sheets on 2 oven racks and bake breadsticks 20 minutes, or until golden and crisp throughout, rotating cookie sheets between upper and lower racks halfway through baking time. Transfer breadsticks to wire racks to cool. Repeat with remaining dough. Makes 64 breadsticks.

Each breadstick: About 50 calories, 1 g protein, 7 g carbohydrate, 2 g total fat (0 g saturated), 0 mg cholesterol, 85 mg sodium.

◆ *Arrabbiata Sauce,*
Rosemary-Fennel Breadsticks,
and Marinated Olives

HOT AND SWEET NUT BRITTLE

PREP: 20 MINUTES
COOK: ABOUT 30 MINUTES

1 pound blanched whole almonds
¼ cup cider vinegar
2 cups plus 1 tablespoon sugar
2 teaspoons salt
2 teaspoons ground cumin
1 teaspoon ground coriander
½ to ¾ teaspoon ground red pepper (cayenne)

1. Preheat oven to 375°F. Place almonds in 15 ½" by 10 ½" jelly-roll pan. Bake, shaking pan occasionally, 10 to 15 minutes, until golden brown. Cool almonds in pan on wire rack.

2. While almonds cool, in heavy 3-quart saucepan, heat vinegar and 2 cups sugar to boiling over medium heat. Continue cooking over medium heat, stirring occasionally, 15 to 20 minutes, until mixture turns dark amber in color. (If using a candy thermometer, temperature should read about 360°F.)

3. Meanwhile, in small bowl, mix salt, cumin, coriander, ground red pepper, and remaining 1 tablespoon sugar. Lightly grease large cookie sheet.

4. Remove saucepan from heat. Stir spice mixture into hot sugar syrup. Add almonds and stir until evenly coated. Immediately pour mixture onto cookie sheet. With 2 forks, spread almond mixture to form a single layer.

5. Cool brittle completely on cookie sheet on wire rack. With hands, break brittle into small pieces. Store in tightly covered jar or tin up to 1 month. Makes about 1 ¾ pounds.

Each ounce: About 145 calories, 4 g protein, 18 g carbohydrate, 8 g total fat (1 g saturated), 0 mg cholesterol, 155 mg sodium.

CHOCOLATE TRUFFLES

PREP: 25 MINUTES PLUS CHILLING

8 ounces bittersweet chocolate
½ cup heavy or whipping cream
3 tablespoons unsalted butter, softened and cut up
  (do not use margarine)
⅓ cup hazelnuts (filberts), toasted and
  finely chopped
3 tablespoons unsweetened cocoa

1. In food processor with knife blade attached, process chocolate until finely ground.

2. In 1-quart saucepan, heat heavy cream over medium-high heat to boiling. Add cream to chocolate in food processor and blend until smooth. Add butter and blend well.

3. Line 9" by 5" metal loaf pan with plastic wrap. Pour chocolate mixture into pan; spread evenly. Refrigerate about 3 hours, until cool and firm enough to handle.

4. Remove chocolate mixture from pan by lifting edges of plastic wrap and inverting chocolate block onto cutting board; discard plastic wrap. Cut chocolate block into 32 pieces. (To cut chocolate mixture easily, dip knife in hot water and wipe dry.) Quickly roll each piece into a ball. Roll half of balls in chopped hazelnuts and roll other half of balls in cocoa. Refrigerate truffles in airtight containers up to 1 week or freeze up to 1 month. Remove from freezer 5 minutes before serving. Makes 32 truffles.

Each truffle: About 65 calories, 1 g protein, 5 g carbohydrate, 6 g total fat (3 g saturated), 8 mg cholesterol, 2 mg sodium.

PEANUT BUTTER CUPS

PREP: 40 MINUTES PLUS CHILLING

> 9 ounces white chocolate or 1½ packages
>   (6 ounces each) white baking bars, chopped
> 1½ cups creamy peanut butter
> 1 package (8 ounces) semisweet chocolate squares,
>   chopped
> ⅓ cup lightly salted cocktail peanuts, chopped

1. Arrange 60 miniature (1" by ¼") paper or foil baking cups on 15½" by 10½" jelly-roll pan.

2. In heavy 2-quart saucepan, heat chopped white chocolate and ¼ cup peanut butter over low heat, stirring occasionally, until melted and smooth. Spoon peanut-butter mixture into baking cups. Refrigerate 10 minutes.

3. Meanwhile, in heavy 2-quart saucepan, heat chopped semisweet chocolate and remaining 1¼ cups peanut butter over low heat, stirring occasionally, until melted and smooth.

4. Spoon warm chocolate-peanut butter mixture over chilled mixture in baking cups; sprinkle with peanuts. Refrigerate overnight. Store candies, covered, in refrigerator up to 1 week or in air-tight container in freezer up to 1 month. Makes 60 candies.

Each candy: About 85 calories, 2 g protein, 7 g carbohydrate, 6 g total fat (2 g saturated), 1 mg cholesterol, 40 mg sodium.

PEAR CHUTNEY

PREP: 30 MINUTES
COOK: ABOUT 15 MINUTES

> 12 ounces dried pear halves, chopped (2 cups)
> 1 large red onion, finely chopped (1 cup)
> 2½ cups pear nectar
> 2 cups dark seedless and/or golden raisins
> ¾ cup cider vinegar
> ½ cup dried tart cherries
> ⅓ cup sugar
> 1 tablespoon mustard seeds
> 1 tablespoon grated, peeled fresh ginger
> ¼ teaspoon salt
> 1 cinnamon stick (3 inches)
> 1 cup water

1. In 4-quart saucepan, combine all ingredients and heat to boiling over high heat, stirring occasionally. Reduce heat; simmer, uncovered, 15 minutes, or until pears are very soft, stirring frequently.

2. Discard cinnamon stick. Spoon chutney into jars; cover tightly. Store in refrigerator up to 1 month. Makes about 6 cups.

Each ¼ cup: About 115 calories, 1 g protein, 30 g carbohydrate, 0 g total fat, 0 mg cholesterol, 25 mg sodium.

◆ *Your jars of delicious homemade sauces and preserves or baskets of scrumptious baked goodies deserve special attention when you wrap them for gifts. Enclose them in layers of colored cellophane or tulle sparkled with spray-on glitter. Use wide grosgrain, wired organza, or velvet ribbon for pretty bows—or go for the natural look with easy-to-handle raffia. Loop the bow around a cookie cutter, or a bundle of cinnamon sticks, or a spray of pepper berries for a touch of whimsy.*

OLD-FASHIONED FRUIT CAKES

PREP: 40 MINUTES PLUS STANDING
BAKE: 60 TO 70 MINUTES

2 cups dark seedless raisins
1 cup dried apricots, coarsely chopped
1 cup dried Calimyrna figs, coarsely chopped
1 cup pitted dates, coarsely chopped
1 cup brandy
2 ½ cups all-purpose flour
1 teaspoon baking powder
1 teaspoon salt
1 teaspoon ground cinnamon
½ teaspoon baking soda
½ teaspoon ground nutmeg
½ teaspoon ground allspice
1 ¼ cups packed light brown sugar
1 cup butter or margarine (2 sticks), softened
5 large eggs
¼ cup light molasses
1 teaspoon grated orange peel
2 cups coarsely chopped walnuts or pecans

1. In large bowl, combine raisins, apricots, figs, dates, and ¾ cup brandy; toss to combine. Cover and let stand 4 hours or overnight.

2. Preheat oven to 300°F. Grease six 5 ¾" by 3 ¼" loaf pans; line bottoms with waxed paper; grease paper. Dust with flour. In medium bowl, combine flour, baking powder, salt, cinnamon, baking soda, nutmeg, and allspice; set aside.

3. In another large bowl, with mixer at low speed, beat brown sugar with butter until blended. Increase speed to high; beat until light and creamy. At low speed, add eggs, 1 at a time, beating well after each addition. Add molasses, orange peel, and flour mixture and beat until blended. With spoon, stir in dried-fruit mixture and nuts.

4. Spoon batter evenly into pans. On bottom oven rack, pour *boiling water* into roasting pan to fill

◆ *Old-Fashioned Fruit Cake*

halfway. Place fruitcakes on rack above. Bake fruitcakes 60 to 70 minutes, until tops are golden and toothpick inserted in center comes out clean with a few moist crumbs attached.

5. Cool fruitcakes in pans on wire rack 30 minutes. Remove from pans; discard waxed paper. Brush remaining ¼ cup brandy over tops of warm cakes. Cool completely. Wrap each fruitcake well with plastic wrap or foil. Store at room temperature up to 1 week or refrigerate up to 1 month. Makes 6 small (12-ounce) fruitcakes, each 8 servings.

Each serving: About 175 calories, 3 g protein, 25 g carbohydrate, 8 g total fat (1 g saturated), 22 mg cholesterol, 125 mg sodium.

BUTTERSCOTCH SAUCE

PREP: 5 MINUTES
COOK: 10 MINUTES

4 cups packed light brown sugar
2 cups heavy or whipping cream
1 ⅓ cups light corn syrup
½ cup butter or margarine (1 stick)
4 teaspoons distilled white vinegar
½ teaspoon salt
4 teaspoons vanilla extract

1. In 5-quart Dutch oven (do not use smaller pot because mixture bubbles up during cooking), combine brown sugar, heavy cream, corn syrup, butter, vinegar, and salt; heat to boiling over high heat, stirring occasionally. Reduce heat; simmer, uncovered, stirring frequently, 5 minutes.

2. Remove Dutch oven from heat; stir in vanilla. Sauce will have thin consistency when hot but will thicken when chilled. Cool sauce completely. Transfer to jars with tight-fitting lids. Store in refrigerator up to 2 weeks. Reheat to serve warm over ice cream. Makes about 6 cups.

Each tablespoon: About 75 calories, 0 g protein, 13 g carbohydrate, 3 g total fat (1 g saturated), 7 mg cholesterol, 35 mg sodium.

Cookies

GREAT-GRANNY'S OLD-TIME SPICE COOKIES

PREP: 1 HOUR 10 MINUTES PLUS CHILLING,
    COOLING, AND DECORATING
BAKE: 8 TO 10 MINUTES PER BATCH

5 ½ cups all-purpose flour
1 teaspoon ground cinnamon
1 teaspoon ground allspice
½ teaspoon ground nutmeg
½ teaspoon baking soda
½ teaspoon salt
1 cup butter or margarine (2 sticks), softened
1 ¼ cups packed light brown sugar
1 jar (12 ounces) dark molasses
Ornamental Frosting (see below), optional

1. In large bowl, combine flour, cinnamon, allspice, nutmeg, baking soda, and salt. In another large bowl, with mixer at low speed, beat butter with brown sugar until blended. Increase speed to high; beat until light and creamy. At low speed, beat in molasses until blended, then beat in 3 cups flour mixture. With spoon, stir in remaining flour mixture. Divide dough into 4 equal pieces. Wrap each piece in plastic wrap and freeze at least 1 hour or refrigerate overnight, until dough is firm enough to roll.

2. Preheat oven to 350°F. On well-floured surface, with floured rolling pin, roll out 1 piece of dough ⅛ inch thick, keeping remaining dough refrigerated (dough will be soft). With floured 3- to 4-inch assorted cookie cutters, cut dough into as many cookies as possible; reserve trimmings. Place cookies, about 1 inch apart, on ungreased large cookie sheet.

3. Bake cookies 8 to 10 minutes, just until browned. Cool cookies on cookie sheet 5 minutes. With wide spatula, transfer cookies to wire rack to cool completely. Repeat with remaining dough and trimmings.

4. When cookies are cool, prepare Ornamental Frosting, if you like; use to decorate cookies as desired. Set cookies aside to allow frosting to dry completely, about 1 hour. Makes about 4 dozen cookies.

Each cookie without frosting: About 120 calories, 2 g protein, 21 g carbohydrate, 4 g total fat (1 g saturated), 0 mg cholesterol, 95 mg sodium.

ORNAMENTAL FROSTING: In bowl, with mixer at medium speed, beat 1 package (16 ounces) confectioners' sugar, 3 tablespoons meringue powder (see Sources, page 156), and ⅓ cup warm water about 5 minutes, until blended and mixture is so stiff that knife drawn through it leaves a clean-cut path. If you like, tint frosting with food colorings or food-color pastes; keep covered with plastic wrap to prevent drying out. With small metal spatula, artist's paintbrushes, or decorating bags with small writing tips, decorate cookies with frosting. (You may need to thin frosting with a little warm water.) Makes about 3 cups.

Each tablespoon: About 40 calories, 0 g protein, 10 g carbohydrate, 0 g total fat (0 g saturated), 0 mg cholesterol, 3 mg sodium.

◆ *Clockwise from top of plate: Great Granny's Old-Time Spice Cookies, Sand Tarts, and Jelly Centers.*

SAND TARTS

PREP: 1 HOUR 30 MINUTES PLUS CHILLING,
    COOLING, AND DECORATING
BAKE: 12 TO 15 MINUTES PER BATCH

1 cup butter (2 sticks), softened (do not
    use margarine)
1½ cups sugar
2 large eggs
1 teaspoon vanilla extract
3 cups all-purpose flour
½ teaspoon baking powder
½ teaspoon salt
Ornamental Frosting (see page 128), optional

1. In large bowl, with mixer at low speed, beat butter with sugar until blended. Increase speed to high; beat until light and creamy. At low speed, beat in eggs and vanilla until mixed, then beat in flour, baking powder, and salt, occasionally scraping bowl with rubber spatula, until well combined. Shape dough into 4 balls; flatten each slightly. Wrap each ball in plastic wrap and freeze at least 1 hour or refrigerate overnight, until dough is firm enough to roll.

2. Preheat oven to 350°F. On lightly floured surface, with floured rolling pin, roll out 1 piece of dough slightly thinner than ¼ inch, keeping remaining dough refrigerated. With floured 3- to 4-inch assorted cookie cutters, cut dough into as many cookies as possible; reserve trimmings. Place cookies, about 1 inch apart, on ungreased large cookie sheet.

3. Bake cookies 12 to 15 minutes, until golden around edges. With wide spatula, transfer cookies to wire rack to cool. Repeat with remaining dough and trimmings.

4. When cookies are cool, prepare Ornamental Frosting, if you like; use to decorate cookies as desired. Set cookies aside to allow frosting to dry completely, about 1 hour. Makes about 6 dozen cookies.

Each cookie without frosting: About 60 calories, 1 g protein, 8 g carbohydrate, 3 g total fat (2 g saturated), 13 mg cholesterol, 45 mg sodium.

JELLY CENTERS

PREP: 45 MINUTES PLUS CHILLING AND COOLING
BAKE: 10 TO 12 MINUTES PER BATCH

1 cup butter or margarine (2 sticks), softened
1¼ cups sugar
2 large eggs, separated
2 teaspoons vanilla extract
3 cups all-purpose flour
⅛ teaspoon baking powder
⅛ teaspoon salt
about 1 cup raspberry preserves

1. In large bowl, with mixer at low speed, beat butter with 1 cup sugar, occasionally scraping bowl with rubber spatula, until blended. Increase speed to high; beat until light and fluffy. At low speed, beat in egg yolks and vanilla until blended. Gradually beat in flour, baking powder, and salt. Shape dough into 2 balls; flatten each slightly. Wrap each in plastic wrap; refrigerate 1 hour or until firm enough to roll.

2. Preheat oven to 350°F. Between 2 sheets of floured waxed paper, roll out half of dough ⅛ inch thick, keeping remaining dough refrigerated. With floured 2-inch cookie cutter, cut out as many cookies as possible. Place cookies, ½ inch apart, on ungreased large cookie sheet; reserve trimmings. With ½-inch round or star-shaped cookie cutter, cut out centers from half of cookies. Remove centers; add to trimmings.

3. In cup, beat egg whites slightly. Brush cookies with cut-out centers with some egg white, then sprinkle with some of remaining ¼ cup sugar. Bake all cookies 10 to 12 minutes, until cookies are lightly browned. Transfer cookies to wire rack to cool.

4. Repeat steps 2 and 3 to make more cookies.

5. When cookies are cool, spread center of each cookie without cut-out center with ¼ to ½ teaspoon jam; top each with a cookie with a cut-out center, gently pressing cookies together to form a sandwich. Makes about 4½ dozen sandwich cookies.

Each sandwich cookie: About 95 calories, 1 g protein, 14 g carbohydrate, 4 g total fat (1 g saturated), 8 mg cholesterol, 55 mg sodium.

◆ *From left: Aunt Tess's Anisette Cookies, Good Housekeeping Gingerbread Cutouts, and Layered Date Bars*

LAYERED DATE BARS

PREP: 30 MINUTES PLUS COOLING
BAKE: 40 MINUTES

> 1 package (10 ounces) pitted dates (2 cups),
>   coarsely chopped
> ½ cup walnuts, finely chopped
> ¼ cup sugar
> 1 ¼ cups water
> 1 ½ cups all-purpose flour
> 1 ½ cups old-fashioned oats, uncooked
> 1 cup packed brown sugar
> 1 teaspoon baking soda
> ¾ cup butter or margarine (1 ½ sticks),
>   softened

1. Preheat oven to 350°F. In 2-quart saucepan, combine dates, walnuts, sugar, and water and heat to boiling over high heat. Reduce heat; simmer, uncovered, stirring occasionally, 10 to 15 minutes, until dates are soft and mixture is thick. Set aside.

2. Meanwhile, in large bowl, combine flour, oats, brown sugar, and baking soda. With hand, knead in butter until dough forms. Press half of dough evenly in bottom of 13" by 9" metal baking pan. Bake 15 minutes, or until pale golden.

3. Spread date mixture evenly over hot crust. Sprinkle remaining oat mixture on top. Bake 25 minutes longer, or until golden. Cool completely in pan on wire rack. When cool, cut lengthwise into 4 strips, then cut each strip crosswise into 8 pieces. Makes 32 bars.

Each bar: About 155 calories, 2 g protein, 25 g carbohydrate, 6 g total fat (1 g saturated), 0 mg cholesterol, 100 mg sodium.

AUNT TESS'S ANISETTE COOKIES

PREP: 1 HOUR PLUS CHILLING AND COOLING
BAKE: 12 MINUTES PER BATCH

½ cup butter or margarine (1 stick), softened
½ cup granulated sugar
3 large eggs
1 teaspoon vanilla extract
2 teaspoons anise extract or anisette
2½ cups all-purpose flour
1 tablespoon baking powder
¾ cup confectioners' sugar
2 tablespoons water
red and green sprinkles (optional)

1. In large bowl, with mixer at low speed, beat butter with granulated sugar until blended. Increase speed to high, beat until creamy. At medium speed, beat in eggs, vanilla, and 1 teaspoon anise extract, constantly scraping bowl with rubber spatula. Reduce speed to low; beat in flour and baking powder, occasionally scraping bowl, until blended. Shape dough into 4 balls. Wrap each ball in plastic wrap and freeze at least 1 hour or refrigerate overnight.

2. Preheat oven to 350°F. On lightly floured surface, divide 1 ball of dough into 9 equal pieces, keeping remaining dough refrigerated. With lightly floured hands, roll each piece of dough into a 7-inch-long rope; bring ends of rope together and gently twist several times. Pinch twisted ends together to seal.

3. Place cookies, 2 inches apart, on ungreased large cookie sheet. Bake cookies 12 minutes, or until bottoms are lightly browned. Transfer cookies to wire rack to cool. Repeat with remaining dough.

4. When cookies are cool, prepare glaze: In small bowl, mix confectioners' sugar with remaining 1 teaspoon anise extract and water. Brush cookies with glaze; place on rack. Top with sprinkles, if you like. Allow glaze to dry, about 1 hour. Makes 3 dozen cookies.

Each cookie without sprinkles: About 80 calories, 1 g protein, 12 g carbohydrate, 3 g total fat (1 g saturated), 18 mg cholesterol, 70 mg sodium.

GOOD HOUSEKEEPING GINGERBREAD CUTOUTS

PREP: 45 MINUTES PLUS COOLING AND
    DECORATING
BAKE: 12 MINUTES PER BATCH

½ cup sugar
½ cup light molasses
1½ teaspoons ground ginger
1 teaspoon ground allspice
1 teaspoon ground cinnamon
1 teaspoon ground cloves
2 teaspoons baking soda
½ cup butter or margarine (1 stick),
    cut into pieces
1 large egg, beaten
3½ cups all-purpose flour
Ornamental Frosting (see page 128)

1. In 3-quart saucepan, combine sugar, molasses, ginger, allspice, cinnamon, and cloves and heat to boiling over medium heat, stirring occasionally. Remove saucepan from heat; stir in baking soda (mixture will foam up in the pan). Add butter and stir until melted. With fork, stir in egg, then flour. On floured surface, knead dough until well combined. Divide dough in half; wrap half in plastic wrap and set aside.

2. Preheat oven to 325°F. With floured rolling pin, roll out remaining half of dough slightly thinner than ¼ inch. With floured 3- to 4-inch assorted cookie cutters, cut dough into cookies; reserve trimmings. Place cookies, 1 inch apart, on ungreased cookie sheet. Reroll trimmings and cut out more cookies.

3. Bake 12 minutes, or until edges begin to brown. Transfer to wire racks. Repeat with remaining dough.

4. When cookies are cool, prepare Ornamental Frosting; use to decorate cookies as desired. Set cookies aside to allow frosting to dry completely, about 1 hour. If not serving right away, store cookies in airtight container. Makes about 3 dozen cookies.

Each cookie without frosting: About 90 calories, 1 g protein, 15 g carbohydrate, 3 g total fat (1 g saturated), 6 mg cholesterol, 105 mg sodium.

PENNSYLVANIA-DUTCH BROWNIES

PREP: 20 MINUTES PLUS COOLING
BAKE: 15 TO 20 MINUTES

4 tablespoons butter or margarine
1 square (1 ounce) unsweetened chocolate
¼ cup light molasses
2 large eggs
1½ cups all-purpose flour
1 teaspoon ground ginger
½ teaspoon ground cloves
½ teaspoon baking soda
½ teaspoon salt
1 cup plus 2 teaspoons sugar
1⅛ teaspoons ground cinnamon

1. Preheat oven to 375°F. Grease 13" by 9" metal baking pan; set aside.

2. In 4-quart saucepan, melt butter with chocolate over low heat. Remove saucepan from heat. With wire whisk or fork, stir in molasses, then eggs.

3. With spoon, stir in flour, ginger, cloves, baking soda, salt, 1 cup sugar, and 1 teaspoon cinnamon just until blended. Spread batter evenly in pan. Bake 15 to 20 minutes, until toothpick inserted 2 inches from edge comes out clean.

4. Meanwhile, in cup, combine remaining 2 teaspoons sugar and ⅛ teaspoon cinnamon; set aside.

5. Remove pan from oven; immediately sprinkle brownies with cinnamon-sugar mixture. Cool brownies in pan on wire rack at least 2 hours. When cool, cut brownies lengthwise into 3 strips, then cut each strip crosswise into 5 pieces. Cut each piece diagonally in half. Makes 30 brownies.

Each brownie: About 80 calories, 1 g protein, 14 g carbohydrate, 2 g total fat (1 g saturated), 14 mg cholesterol, 80 mg sodium.

MISS ELSIE'S ALMOND SLICES

PREP: 45 MINUTES PLUS FREEZING
  AND COOLING
BAKE: 15 MINUTES PER BATCH

1½ cups butter (3 sticks), melted (do not
  use margarine)
1 cup packed light brown sugar
1 cup granulated sugar
3 large eggs
1 teaspoon vanilla extract
½ teaspoon lemon extract
1 cup slivered almonds, finely ground
5½ cups all-purpose flour
2 teaspoons ground cinnamon
1½ teaspoons baking soda
1 teaspoon salt
1 teaspoon ground nutmeg

1. In large bowl, with spoon, combine melted butter and sugars. Add eggs, vanilla, lemon extract, and ground almonds; beat until well combined. Add flour, cinnamon, baking soda, salt, and nutmeg and stir until dough forms. Cover bowl with plastic wrap and freeze dough 1 hour, or until easy to handle.

2. Divide dough into 8 pieces. On lightly floured surface, with floured hands, shape each piece into a 6-inch-long log. Wrap each log in plastic wrap and freeze at least 4 hours or overnight, until firm enough to slice.

3. Preheat oven to 350°F. Grease large cookie sheet. Cut logs into very thin (about 3/16-inch) slices. Place slices, 1½ inches apart, on cookie sheet. Bake 15 minutes, or until cookies are browned. With wide spatula, transfer cookies to wire rack to cool. Makes about 24 dozen cookies.

Each cookie: About 25 calories, 0 g protein, 3 g carbohydrate, 1 g total fat (0 g saturated), 5 mg cholesterol, 25 mg sodium.

MOM'S PFEFFERNUSSE

PREP: 1 HOUR 30 MINUTES PLUS CHILLING
  AND COOLING
BAKE: 8 TO 10 MINUTES PER BATCH

2 cups sugar
4 large eggs
3½ cups all-purpose flour
2 tablespoons grated orange peel
1 teaspoon ground cinnamon
1 teaspoon ground allspice
1 teaspoon baking powder
1 teaspoon lemon extract
½ teaspoon ground cloves

1. In large bowl, with mixer at low speed, beat sugar and eggs until blended. Increase speed to high; beat until creamy. Reduce speed to low; add flour, grated orange peel, cinnamon, allspice, baking powder, lemon extract, and cloves and beat, occasionally scraping bowl with rubber spatula, until well combined. With lightly floured hands, shape dough into 4 balls; flatten each slightly. Wrap each in plastic wrap and freeze 1 hour or refrigerate overnight. (Dough will be very sticky even after chilling.)

2. Preheat oven to 400°F. Grease large cookie sheet. On well-floured surface, with floured rolling pin, roll out 1 piece of dough into 10" by 6" rectangle, keeping remaining dough in refrigerator. With floured pastry wheel or sharp knife, cut dough lengthwise into 6 strips, then cut each strip crosswise into 10 pieces. Place cookies, about ½ inch apart, on cookie sheet.

3. Bake cookies 8 to 10 minutes, until lightly browned. With wide spatula, transfer cookies to wire racks to cool. Repeat with remaining dough. Makes 20 dozen cookies.

Each cookie: About 15 calories, 0 g protein, 3 g carbohydrate, 0 g total fat, 4 mg cholesterol, 5 mg sodium.

◆ *Clockwise from top left: Pennsylvania-Dutch Brownies, Miss Elsie's Almond Slices, Honey Cookies, Christmas Rocks, and Mom's Pfeffernusse*

CHRISTMAS ROCKS

PREP: 45 MINUTES PLUS COOLING
BAKE: 12 TO 15 MINUTES PER BATCH

½ cup packed brown sugar
⅓ cup shortening
6 tablespoons butter or margarine, softened
2 large eggs
1½ cups all-purpose flour
1 teaspoon baking powder
1 teaspoon ground cinnamon
½ teaspoon baking soda
½ teaspoon salt
¼ teaspoon ground cloves
2 cups walnuts, coarsely chopped
2 cups dark seedless raisins
½ cup dried currants
½ cup red and/or green candied cherries,
  each cut in half
½ cup finely chopped candied pineapple

1. In large bowl, with mixer at low speed, beat brown sugar, shortening, and butter, occasionally scraping bowl with rubber spatula, until mixed. Increase speed to high; beat mixture until creamy, about 2 minutes.

2. With mixer at low speed, beat in eggs, then flour, baking powder, cinnamon, baking soda, salt, and cloves just until mixed. With spoon, stir in walnuts and remaining ingredients.

3. Preheat oven to 350°F. Drop dough by rounded tablespoons, about 1½ inches apart, on ungreased large cookie sheet. Bake 12 to 15 minutes, until set and lightly browned. With wide spatula, transfer cookies to wire rack to cool. Repeat with remaining dough. Makes about 4 dozen cookies.

Each cookie: About 120 calories, 2 g protein, 16 g carbohydrate, 6 g total fat (1 g saturated), 9 mg cholesterol, 70 mg sodium.

HONEY COOKIES

PREP: 40 MINUTES PLUS CHILLING AND COOLING
BAKE: 18 TO 22 MINUTES PER BATCH

1 cup butter or margarine (2 sticks), softened
¼ cup honey
2 teaspoons vanilla extract
2 cups all-purpose flour
2 cups walnuts, chopped
½ teaspoon salt

1. In large bowl, with mixer at high speed, beat butter until creamy. Add honey and vanilla; beat until well blended.

2. With mixer at low speed, beat in flour, walnuts, and salt until dough forms. Cover bowl with plastic wrap and refrigerate dough at least 1 hour.

3. Preheat oven to 325°F. With lightly floured hands, shape dough by heaping teaspoons into balls. Place balls, about 2 inches apart, on ungreased large cookie sheet. Press floured 4-tine fork across top of each ball to make decorative indentations.

4. Bake cookies 18 to 22 minutes, until golden. Transfer to wire rack to cool. Repeat with remaining dough. Makes about 3 ½ dozen cookies.

Each cookie: About 105 calories, 1 g protein, 7 g carbohydrate, 8 g total fat (1 g saturated), 0 mg cholesterol, 85 mg sodium.

◆ *A one-time investment in nonstick cookie sheets will pay off in easy cleaning and fast, even baking. Pick the largest sheets that will fit in your oven, allowing 2 inches of clearance on all sides for good air circulation.*

PEANUTTY YUMMY BARS

PREP: 30 MINUTES
BAKE: 55 MINUTES

⅓ cup quick-cooking oats, uncooked
1⅔ cups all-purpose flour
⅓ cup plus 1½ cups packed light brown sugar
½ cup butter or margarine (1 stick), softened
3 tablespoons plus ⅓ cup chunky peanut butter
3 large eggs
4½ teaspoons light molasses
2 teaspoons baking powder
½ teaspoon salt
1 cup salted cocktail peanuts, chopped
1 package (6 ounces) semisweet chocolate pieces
*   (1 cup)*
confectioners' sugar for garnish (optional)

1. Preheat oven to 350°F. Grease 13" by 9" metal baking pan.

2. Prepare crust: In large bowl, with mixer at low speed, beat oats, 1 cup flour, ⅓ cup brown sugar, 4 tablespoons butter, and 3 tablespoons peanut butter until blended. Pat dough evenly into pan and bake 15 minutes.

3. Meanwhile, in large bowl, with mixer at medium speed, beat eggs, molasses, remaining 1½ cups brown sugar, ⅓ cup peanut butter, and 4 tablespoons butter, constantly scraping bowl with rubber spatula, until well combined. Reduce speed to low; add baking powder, salt, and remaining ⅔ cup flour and beat, occasionally scraping bowl, until blended. With spoon, stir in peanuts and chocolate pieces.

4. Spread mixture evenly over hot crust. Bake 40 minutes longer, or until golden. Cool in pan on wire rack. Dust with confectioners' sugar, if you like. When cool, cut lengthwise into 4 strips, then cut each strip crosswise into 12 pieces. Makes 4 dozen bars.

Each bar: About 125 calories, 3 g protein, 16 g carbohydrate, 6 g total fat (1 g saturated), 13 mg cholesterol, 100 mg sodium.

◆ *Clockwise from left: Colorful Holiday Cookies, Peanutty Yummy Bars, and Sally Ann Cookies*

COLORFUL HOLIDAY COOKIES

PREP: 45 MINUTES PLUS CHILLING AND COOLING
BAKE: 15 TO 17 MINUTES PER BATCH

*1 cup butter or margarine (2 sticks),
  slightly softened*
½ cup packed light brown sugar
½ cup granulated sugar
2 large eggs
3 cups all-purpose flour
½ teaspoon baking soda
½ cup walnuts, coarsely chopped
½ cup pecans, coarsely chopped
½ cup Brazil nuts or almonds, coarsely chopped
½ cup coarsely chopped pitted dates
¼ cup red candied cherries
¼ cup coarsely chopped candied pineapple

1. In large bowl, with mixer at low speed, beat butter with sugars, occasionally scraping bowl with rubber spatula, until blended. Increase speed to high; beat until light and fluffy, about 3 minutes. At low speed, beat in eggs until blended. Gradually beat in flour and baking soda just until mixed. With spoon, stir in walnuts and remaining ingredients.

2. Divide dough into 3 equal pieces. With floured hands, shape each piece into an 8-inch-long log. Wrap each log in plastic wrap and freeze at least 4 hours or overnight, until firm enough to slice.

3. Preheat oven to 350°F. With serrated knife, cut 1 log crosswise into about 24 slices. Place slices, about 2 inches apart, on ungreased large cookie sheet. Bake 15 to 17 minutes, until cookies are golden. With wide spatula, transfer cookies to wire rack to cool. Repeat with remaining logs. Makes about 6 dozen cookies.

Each cookie: About 80 calories, 1 g protein, 9 g carbohydrate, 4 g total fat (1 g saturated), 5 mg cholesterol, 45 mg sodium.

SALLY ANN COOKIES

PREP: I HOUR PLUS FREEZING AND COOLING
BAKE: 15 TO 20 MINUTES PER BATCH

1½ cups granulated sugar
1 cup butter or margarine (2 sticks)
5½ cups all-purpose flour
1 cup light molasses
½ cup cold strong coffee
2 teaspoons baking soda
2 teaspoons ground ginger
½ teaspoon ground nutmeg
½ teaspoon salt
¼ teaspoon ground cloves
holiday décors (optional)

SALLY ANN FROSTING

1 cup granulated sugar
1 envelope unflavored gelatin
1 cup cold water
2 cups confectioners' sugar
¼ teaspoon vanilla extract

1. In large bowl, with mixer at low speed, beat sugar with butter until blended. Increase speed to high; beat until creamy. At low speed, beat in flour and remaining ingredients, except frosting and décors, until well blended. Cover bowl with plastic wrap and freeze 1 hour, or until firm enough to handle.

2. Divide dough into thirds. On lightly floured surface, shape each third into a 12-inch-long log. Wrap each log in plastic wrap and freeze at least 4 hours or overnight, until firm enough to slice.

3. Preheat oven to 350°F. Grease large cookie sheet. Cut 1 log into ¼-inch-thick slices. Place slices, about 1½ inches apart, on cookie sheet. Bake 15 to 20 minutes, until set and lightly browned around edges. Cool on cookie sheet 1 minute. With wide spatula, transfer cookies to wire rack to cool completely. Repeat with remaining dough.

4. When cookies are cool, prepare Sally Ann Frosting: In 2-quart saucepan, combine granulated sugar and gelatin and stir until well mixed. Stir in water; heat to boiling over high heat. Reduce heat; simmer, uncovered, 10 minutes.

5. Into small bowl, pour confectioners' sugar. With mixer at low speed, gradually add gelatin mixture to sugar and beat until well blended. Increase speed to high; beat until smooth and fluffy, with an easy spreading consistency, about 10 minutes. Beat in vanilla extract. Keep bowl covered with plastic wrap to prevent frosting from drying out.

6. With small metal spatula or knife, spread frosting on cookies. If you like, sprinkle cookies with décors. Set cookies aside to allow frosting to dry completely, about 1 hour. Makes about 12 dozen cookies.

Each cookie without décors: About 55 calories, 0 g protein, 10 g carbohydrate, 1 g total fat (0 g saturated), 0 mg cholesterol, 40 mg sodium.

♦ *If you would like to use* Good Housekeeping *Gingerbread Cutouts or Noël Sugar Cookies as ornaments, make 1 or 2 holes in the top of each cookie with a toothpick or straw before baking. If the holes fill in during baking, remake the holes while the cookies are still warm. After decorating, loop nylon fishing line or ribbon through for hanging.*

NOËL SUGAR COOKIES

PREP: 45 MINUTES PLUS CHILLING, COOLING,
    AND DECORATING
BAKE: 12 TO 15 MINUTES PER BATCH

¾ cup sugar
10 tablespoons butter (1 ¼ sticks), softened
1 teaspoon baking powder
½ teaspoon salt
2 tablespoons milk
2 teaspoons vanilla extract
1 large egg
2 cups all-purpose flour
Ornamental Frosting (see page 128)

1. In large bowl, with mixer at low speed, beat sugar, butter, baking powder, and salt until blended. Increase speed to high; beat until light and fluffy. Reduce speed to low; add milk, vanilla, and egg and beat until blended. (Mixture may appear curdled.)

2. With wooden spoon, stir in flour until blended. Shape dough into 2 balls; flatten each slightly. Wrap each with plastic wrap and refrigerate 1 hour, or until dough is easy to handle. (Or, place dough in freezer 30 minutes.)

3. Preheat oven to 350°F. On lightly floured surface, with floured rolling pin, roll out 1 piece of dough ⅛ inch thick, keeping remaining dough refrigerated. With floured 3- to 4-inch assorted cookie cutters, cut dough into as many cookies as possible; reserve trimmings. Place cookies, about 1 inch apart, on 2 ungreased large cookie sheets. Reroll trimmings and cut out more cookies.

4. Bake cookies on 2 oven racks 12 to 15 minutes, until golden around edges, rotating cookie sheets between upper and lower racks halfway through baking time. With wide spatula, transfer cookies to wire racks to cool. Repeat with remaining dough.

5. When cookies are cool, prepare Ornamental Frosting; use to decorate cookies as desired. Set cookies aside to allow frosting to dry completely, at least 1 hour. If not using right away, store in tightly covered container. Makes about 4 dozen cookies.

Each cookie without frosting: About 55 calories, 1 g protein, 7 g carbohydrate, 3 g total fat (2 g saturated), 11 mg cholesterol, 55 mg sodium.

FINSKA KAKOR

PREP: 1 HOUR PLUS COOLING
BAKE: 17 TO 20 MINUTES PER BATCH

1 cup blanched almonds
2 tablespoons plus ½ cup sugar
4 cups all-purpose flour
1 ½ cups butter or margarine (3 sticks), softened
2 teaspoons almond extract
1 egg white, beaten

1. In food processor with knife blade attached, process almonds with 2 tablespoons sugar until almonds are finely chopped; set aside.

2. Into large bowl, measure flour, butter, almond extract, and remaining ½ cup sugar. With hand, knead ingredients until well blended and mixture holds together.

3. Preheat oven to 350°F. On work surface, between 2 sheets of waxed paper, roll out half of dough into 12" by 8" rectangle. With pastry brush, brush dough rectangle with some egg white. Sprinkle with half of almond mixture. With rolling pin, gently press almonds into dough.

4. Cut dough rectangle lengthwise into 8 strips. Cut each strip crosswise into 4 bars. With wide spatula, place bars, about ½ inch apart, on ungreased large cookie sheet.

5. Bake bars 17 to 20 minutes, until lightly browned. Transfer to wire rack to cool. Repeat with remaining dough. Makes 64 bars.

Each bar: About 85 calories, 1 g protein, 8 g carbohydrate, 5 g total fat (1 g saturated), 0 mg cholesterol, 60 mg sodium.

NOISETTINES

PREP: 1 HOUR PLUS CHILLING AND COOLING
BAKE: 30 MINUTES

> 1 package (3 ounces) cream cheese, softened
> ½ cup (1 stick) plus 1 tablespoon butter or
>   margarine, softened
> 1 cup all-purpose flour
> 1⅓ cups hazelnuts (filberts)
> ⅔ cup packed light brown sugar
> 1 large egg
> 1 teaspoon vanilla extract

1. In large bowl, with mixer at high speed, beat cream cheese with ½ cup butter until creamy. Reduce speed to low; add flour and beat until well combined. Cover bowl with plastic wrap and refrigerate 30 minutes.

2. Meanwhile, preheat oven to 350°F. Place hazelnuts in 9" by 9" metal baking pan. Bake 10 to 15 minutes until toasted. Wrap hot hazelnuts in clean cloth towel. With hands, roll hazelnuts back and forth to remove skins. Cool completely.

3. Reserve 24 hazelnuts for garnish. In food processor with knife blade attached, process remaining hazelnuts with brown sugar until nuts are finely ground.

4. In medium bowl, with spoon, combine hazelnut mixture with egg, vanilla, and remaining 1 tablespoon butter.

5. With floured hands, divide chilled dough into 24 equal pieces (dough will be very soft). Gently press each piece of dough evenly onto bottom and up sides of 24 ungreased miniature muffin-pan cups. Spoon filling by heaping teaspoons into each pastry cup; place 1 whole hazelnut on top of filling in each cup.

6. Bake 30 minutes, or until filling is set and crust is golden. With tip of knife, loosen cookie cups from muffin-pan cups and place on wire rack to cool completely. Makes 2 dozen cookies.

Each cookie: About 135 calories, 2 g protein, 11 g carbohydrate, 10 g total fat (2 g saturated), 13 mg cholesterol, 75 mg sodium.

◆ *Clockwise from top right: Noisettines, Horns, and Finska Kakor*

HORNS

PREP: 1 HOUR 30 MINUTES PLUS FREEZING
   AND COOLING
BAKE: 20 MINUTES PER BATCH

> 1 cup butter or margarine (2 sticks)
> 2½ cups all-purpose flour
> 1 container (8 ounces) sour cream
> 1 large egg yolk
> ¾ cup sugar
> ¾ cup walnuts, finely chopped
> 1½ teaspoons ground cinnamon
> confectioners' sugar for garnish

1. In large bowl, with pastry blender or 2 knives used scissor-fashion, cut butter into flour until fine crumbs form. In cup, with fork, mix sour cream and egg yolk. Stir sour-cream mixture into flour mixture just until blended and dough comes away from side of bowl (dough will be sticky). Cover bowl with plastic wrap and freeze 1 hour, or until firm enough to handle.

2. Divide dough into 5 equal pieces. On lightly floured surface, shape each piece into a disk. Wrap each disk in plastic wrap and freeze at least 4 hours or overnight, until firm enough to roll.

3. In small bowl, combine sugar, walnuts, and cinnamon. On sheet of lightly floured waxed paper, with floured rolling pin, roll out 1 piece of dough into a 12-inch round, keeping remaining dough refrigerated. Sprinkle dough with rounded ¼ cup walnut mixture; gently press into dough. With pastry wheel or sharp knife, cut dough into 16 equal wedges. Starting at curved edge, roll up each wedge, jelly-roll fashion. Place cookies, point side down, 1½ inches apart, on ungreased cookie sheet. Shape each into a crescent. Repeat with remaining dough, one-fifth at a time.

4. Preheat oven to 350°F. Bake cookies 20 minutes, or until golden. With wide spatula, transfer cookies to wire rack to cool. When cookies are cool, sprinkle with confectioners' sugar. Makes 80 cookies.

Each cookie: About 55 calories, 1 g protein, 5 g carbohydrate, 4 g total fat (1 g saturated), 4 mg cholesterol, 30 mg sodium.

GREEK CINNAMON PAXIMADIA

PREP: 1 HOUR PLUS COOLING
BAKE: 50 MINUTES

> ½ cup butter or margarine (1 stick), softened
> ½ cup shortening
> 1½ cups sugar
> 3 large eggs
> 1 tablespoon vanilla extract
> 2 teaspoons baking powder
> ½ teaspoon baking soda
> about 4 cups all-purpose flour
> 1½ teaspoons ground cinnamon

1. In large bowl, with mixer at low speed, beat butter, shortening, and 1 cup sugar until blended. Increase speed to high; beat until light and fluffy, about 5 minutes. At low speed, add eggs, 1 at a time, then vanilla, and beat until well mixed.

2. Gradually add baking powder, baking soda, and 3 cups flour and beat until well blended. With wooden spoon, stir in remaining 1 cup flour until soft dough forms. If necessary, add additional flour (up to ½ cup) until dough is easy to handle.

3. Preheat oven to 350°F. Divide dough into 4 equal pieces. On lightly floured surface, shape each piece of dough into an 8-inch-long log. Place 2 logs, about 4 inches apart, on each of 2 ungreased large cookie sheets. Flatten each log to 2½ inches wide.

4. Place cookie sheets on 2 oven racks and bake logs 20 minutes, or until lightly browned and toothpick inserted in center comes out clean, rotating cookie sheets between upper and lower racks halfway through baking time. Meanwhile, in pie plate, mix cinnamon with remaining ½ cup sugar.

5. Remove cookie sheets from oven. Transfer hot loaves (during baking, logs will spread and become loaves) to cutting board; with serrated knife, cut diagonally into ½-inch-thick slices. Coat slices with cinnamon-sugar. Return slices, cut side down, to same cookie sheets. Bake slices 15 minutes. Turn slices over and return to oven, rotating cookie sheets between upper and lower racks, and bake 15 minutes longer, or until golden. With wide spatula, transfer cookies to wire racks to cool. Makes about 4 dozen cookies.

Each cookie: About 105 calories, 1 g protein, 14 g carbohydrate, 5 g total fat (1 g saturated), 13 mg cholesterol, 60 mg sodium.

VINEGAR COOKIES

PREP: 25 MINUTES PLUS CHILLING AND COOLING
BAKE: 17 TO 20 MINUTES PER BATCH

> 1 cup butter or margarine (2 sticks), softened
> 1 cup sugar
> 1½ cups all-purpose flour
> 1 tablespoon distilled white vinegar
> ½ teaspoon baking soda

1. In large bowl, with mixer at low speed, beat butter with sugar until blended. Increase speed to high; beat until light and fluffy, about 3 minutes. At low speed, beat in flour, vinegar, and baking soda, occasionally scraping bowl with rubber spatula, until mixed. Cover bowl with plastic wrap and refrigerate dough 1 hour, or until easy to handle.

2. Preheat oven to 350°F. Drop dough by rounded teaspoons, about 2 inches apart, onto ungreased large cookie sheet. Bake 17 to 20 minutes, until cookies are set and edges are golden. Let cookies remain on cookie sheet 30 seconds, then with wide spatula, transfer cookies to wire rack to cool completely. Repeat with remaining dough. Makes about 4 dozen cookies.

Each cookie: About 65 calories, 0 g protein, 7 g carbohydrate, 4 g total fat (1 g saturated), 0 mg cholesterol, 50 mg sodium.

◆ *From top right:
Greek Cinnamon Paximadia,
Vinegar Cookies, and
Chocolate Sambuca Cookies*

CHOCOLATE SAMBUCA COOKIES

PREP: 30 MINUTES PLUS CHILLING AND COOLING
BAKE: 10 TO 12 MINUTES PER BATCH

12 squares (1 ounce each) semisweet chocolate
4 tablespoons butter or margarine
3 large eggs
⅓ cup sambuca (anise-flavored liqueur)
1 cup granulated sugar
1 cup blanched almonds, finely ground
⅔ cup all-purpose flour
¾ teaspoon baking soda
⅓ cup confectioners' sugar

1. In 2-quart saucepan, melt chocolate with butter over low heat, stirring frequently. Remove saucepan from heat; cool chocolate mixture slightly.

2. In medium bowl, with wire whisk, mix eggs, sambuca, and ½ cup granulated sugar; blend in chocolate mixture. With spoon, stir ground almonds, flour, and baking soda into chocolate mixture until combined (dough will be very soft). Cover bowl with plastic wrap and refrigerate at least 4 hours or overnight.

3. Preheat oven to 350°F. In small bowl, combine confectioners' sugar and remaining ½ cup granulated sugar. With lightly floured hands, roll dough by rounded tablespoons into balls. Roll balls in sugar mixture to coat. Place balls, about 2 inches apart, on ungreased large cookie sheet. Bake 10 to 12 minutes, until cookies are just set and look puffed and cracked. Let cookies remain on cookie sheet 1 minute to cool slightly. With wide spatula, transfer to wire rack to cool completely. Repeat with remaining dough and sugar mixture. Makes about 4 dozen cookies.

Each cookie: About 85 calories, 2 g protein, 12 g carbohydrate, 4 g total fat (0 g saturated), 13 mg cholesterol, 20 mg sodium.

◆ *Clockwise from right on plate:*
Czechoslovakian Cookies, Hazelnut Cookies,
and Wooden-Spoon Cookies

CZECHOSLOVAKIAN COOKIES

PREP: 25 MINUTES PLUS COOLING
BAKE: 45 TO 50 MINUTES

1 cup butter (2 sticks), softened (do not use margarine)
1 cup sugar
2 large egg yolks
2 cups all-purpose flour
pinch salt
1 cup walnuts, chopped
½ cup strawberry preserves

1. Preheat oven to 350°F. Grease 9" by 9" metal baking pan.

2. In large bowl, with mixer at low speed, beat butter and sugar, occasionally scraping bowl with rubber spatula, until mixed. Increase speed to high; beat until light and fluffy.

3. With mixer at low speed, beat in egg yolks, constantly scraping bowl with rubber spatula, until well combined. Add flour and salt and beat, occasionally scraping bowl, until blended. Stir in walnuts.

4. With lightly floured hands, pat half of dough evenly into bottom of pan. Spread strawberry preserves over dough. With lightly floured hands, pinch off ¾-inch pieces from remaining dough and drop over preserves; do not pat down.

5. Bake 45 to 50 minutes, until golden. Cool completely in pan on wire rack. When cool, cut into 3 strips, then cut each strip crosswise into 10 pieces. Makes 30 bars.

Each bar: About 130 calories, 2 g protein, 11 g carbohydrate, 9 g total fat (4 g saturated), 31 mg cholesterol, 70 mg sodium.

HAZELNUT COOKIES

PREP: 1 HOUR PLUS COOLING
BAKE: 25 MINUTES PER BATCH

2 cups hazelnuts (filberts)
¾ cup sugar
5 large egg whites
⅓ cup all-purpose flour
5 tablespoons butter or margarine, melted and cooled
6 squares (6 ounces) semisweet chocolate, melted and cooled

1. Preheat oven to 350°F. Place nuts in 13" by 9" metal baking pan. Bake 10 to 15 minutes, until toasted. Wrap hot hazelnuts in clean cloth towel. With hands, roll hazelnuts back and forth to remove skins. Cool completely.

2. Turn oven control to 275°F. Grease 2 large cookie sheets. In food processor with knife blade attached, process hazelnuts with ¼ cup sugar until nuts are finely ground.

3. In large bowl, with mixer at high speed, beat egg whites until soft peaks form. Beating at high speed, sprinkle in remaining ½ cup sugar, 1 tablespoon at a time, beating well after each addition until sugar completely dissolves and whites stand in stiff peaks. With rubber spatula, fold in ground hazelnuts, flour, and melted butter or margarine.

4. Drop mixture by rounded teaspoons, about 2 inches apart, onto cookie sheets. Bake cookies on 2 oven racks 25 minutes, rotating cookie sheets between upper and lower racks halfway through baking time, or until cookies are firm and edges are golden. With wide spatula, transfer to wire racks to cool. Repeat with remaining batter.

5. When cookies are cool, with small metal spatula, spread thin layer of melted chocolate onto flat side of half of cookies. Top with remaining cookies, flat side down, to make sandwiches. Spoon remaining chocolate into small zip-tight plastic bag; snip 1 corner of bag to make small hole. Squeeze thin lines of chocolate over cookies. Let stand until set. Makes about 4 dozen sandwich cookies.

Each sandwich cookie: About 75 calories, 1 g protein, 7 g carbohydrate, 5 g total fat (0 g saturated), 0 mg cholesterol, 25 mg sodium.

WOODEN-SPOON COOKIES

PREP: 25 MINUTES PLUS COOLING
BAKE: 5 TO 7 MINUTES PER BATCH

¾ cup blanched almonds, ground
½ cup butter or margarine (1 stick), softened
½ cup sugar
1 tablespoon all-purpose flour
1 tablespoon heavy or whipping cream

1. Preheat oven to 350°F. Grease and flour 2 large cookie sheets. In 2-quart saucepan, combine ground almonds, butter, sugar, flour, and cream. Heat over low heat, stirring occasionally, until butter melts. Keep mixture warm over very low heat.

2. Drop batter by rounded teaspoons, about 3 inches apart, onto cookie sheet. (Do not place more than 6 cookies on sheet because, after baking, cookies must be shaped quickly before they harden.)

3. Bake cookies 5 to 7 minutes, until edges are lightly browned and centers are golden. Let cookies remain on cookie sheet 30 to 60 seconds, until edges are set. With long, flexible metal spatula, flip cookies over quickly so lacy texture will be on outside after rolling. Working as quickly as possible, roll each cookie into a cylinder around handle of wooden spoon; transfer to wire rack. If cookies become too hard to roll, return to oven briefly to soften. As each cookie is shaped, remove from spoon handle; cool on wire rack. Repeat until all batter is used. Makes about 3 dozen cookies.

Each cookie: About 50 calories, 1 g protein, 3 g carbohydrate, 4 g total fat (1 g saturated), 1 mg cholesterol, 35 mg sodium.

RICOTTA-CHEESE COOKIES

PREP: 30 MINUTES PLUS COOLING
BAKE: 15 MINUTES PER BATCH

2 cups granulated sugar
1 cup butter or margarine (2 sticks), softened
1 container (15 ounces) ricotta cheese
2 teaspoons vanilla extract
2 large eggs
4 cups all-purpose flour
2 tablespoons baking powder
1 teaspoons salt
1½ cups confectioners' sugar
3 tablespoons milk
red and green sugar crystals

1. Preheat oven to 350°F. In large bowl, with mixer at low speed, beat granulated sugar with butter until blended. Increase speed to high; beat until light and fluffy, about 5 minutes. At medium speed, beat in ricotta, vanilla, and eggs until well combined. Reduce speed to low. Add flour, baking powder, and salt; beat until dough forms.

2. Drop dough by level tablespoons, about 2 inches apart, onto ungreased large cookie sheet. Bake about 15 minutes, until cookies are very lightly golden (cookies will be soft). Transfer cookies to wire rack to cool. Repeat with remaining dough.

3. When cookies are cool, prepare icing: In small bowl, stir confectioners' sugar and milk until smooth. With small metal spatula or knife, spread icing on cookies; sprinkle with red or green sugar crystals. Set cookies aside to allow icing to dry completely, about 1 hour. Makes about 6 dozen cookies.

Each cookie: About 90 calories, 1 g protein, 14 g carbohydrate, 3 g total fat (1 g saturated), 3 mg cholesterol, 100 mg sodium.

Here are a few simple strategies
to make your holiday cookie-baking fast, efficient, and fun!

- *Pick user-friendly equipment like nonstick cookie sheets and smooth-gliding rolling pins with ball bearings in the handles.*
- *Whip up a batch of dough and divide it into small portions (for faster defrosting). Wrap each portion in foil and place in a labeled, heavy-weight plastic bag. Freeze for up to 2 months. Slice-and-bake cookie dough can be used without defrosting; other doughs require a couple of hours in the refrigerator or on the kitchen counter.*
- *For even faster baking, freeze uncooked drop cookies on their pan, then transfer them to freezer bags. Take out enough to fill a sheet (for a small batch use your toaster oven), let warm to room temperature, then bake.*
- *Start your holiday baking early! Baked, iced, and decorated cookies store well frozen for up to 3 months. To freeze baked cookies, bake them completely, cool, and pack them between layers of waxed paper in airtight freezer containers. To prevent sogginess, don't forget to unwrap them before thawing.*
- *Save clean-up time by lining cookie sheets with foil; it can be greased just as you would the pan. For bar cookies, extend a sheet of foil over the edges of the pan. After cooling, remove the whole batch at once, lifting the foil by its edges and placing it on a cutting board.*
- *Set up a production line—while one batch bakes, cut a sheet of foil and place unbaked cookies on it. When the first batch is done, slide the foil onto a rack, cool the baking sheet slightly and slide the second sheet of foil on to bake.*

CINNAMON TWISTS

PREP: 1 HOUR PLUS CHILLING AND COOLING
BAKE: 15 TO 17 MINUTES PER BATCH

1 package (8 ounces) cream cheese, softened
1 cup butter or margarine (2 sticks), softened
2½ cups all-purpose flour
¾ cup walnuts
1 cup sugar
2 teaspoons ground cinnamon
1 large egg, beaten

1. In large bowl, with mixer at low speed, beat cream cheese with butter, constantly scraping bowl with rubber spatula, until blended. Increase speed to high; beat until light and creamy, about 2 minutes. With mixer at low speed, gradually add 1 cup flour and beat until blended. With spoon, stir in remaining 1½ cups flour until smooth.

2. On lightly floured sheet of plastic wrap, pat dough into a 9" by 9" square. Wrap in plastic wrap and refrigerate 2 hours, or until firm enough to roll.

3. Meanwhile, in food processor with knife blade attached, process walnuts with ¼ cup sugar until walnuts are finely ground. In small bowl, combine cinnamon and remaining ¾ cup sugar with walnut mixture and stir until well blended; set aside.

4. Preheat oven to 400°F. Grease large cookie sheet. On lightly floured sheet of waxed paper, with floured rolling pin, roll out dough square into 11" by 10½" rectangle. With pastry brush, brush some beaten egg over top of dough rectangle; sprinkle with half of walnut mixture. Gently press walnut mixture into dough. Invert dough rectangle, nut side down, onto another sheet of lightly floured waxed paper. Brush with beaten egg; sprinkle with remaining walnut mixture and gently press nut mixture into dough.

◆ *Clockwise from left on plate:*
Cinnamon Twists,
Ricotta-Cheese Cookies,
and Greek Christmas Cookies

5. Cut dough lengthwise into three 3½-inch-wide bars, then crosswise into ½-inch-wide strips to make sixty-six 3½" by ½" strips. Twist each strip twice, then place, 1 inch apart, on cookie sheet.

6. Bake twists 15 to 17 minutes, until lightly browned. With wide spatula, loosen twists from cookie sheet and transfer to wire rack to cool. Repeat with remaining strips. Makes 5½ dozen cookies.

Each cookie: About 75 calories, 1 g protein, 7 g carbohydrate, 5 g total fat (1 g saturated), 7 mg cholesterol, 50 mg sodium.

GREEK CHRISTMAS COOKIES

PREP: 50 MINUTES PLUS COOLING
BAKE: 15 MINUTES PER BATCH

1 cup butter or margarine (2 sticks)
2 cups confectioners' sugar
2 cups all-purpose flour
1 teaspoon ground cinnamon
½ teaspoon ground nutmeg
½ teaspoon ground cloves
⅛ teaspoon salt
1 large egg yolk
2 cups blanched almonds, ground
about 1 cup red candied cherries, each cut in half

1. Preheat oven to 350°F. In large bowl, with mixer at low speed, beat butter with confectioners' sugar until blended. Increase speed to high; beat until light and creamy. At low speed, beat in flour, cinnamon, nutmeg, cloves, salt, and egg yolk. Knead in almonds.

2. Roll dough into 1-inch balls (dough will be crumbly). Place balls, 2 inches apart, on ungreased large cookie sheet. Gently press a cherry half on top of each ball. Bake 15 minutes, or until bottoms of cookies are lightly browned. With wide spatula, transfer cookies to wire rack to cool. Repeat with remaining dough and cherries. Makes about 6 dozen cookies.

Each cookie: About 75 calories, 1 g protein, 9 g carbohydrate, 4 g total fat (1 g saturated), 3 mg cholesterol, 40 mg sodium.

Children's Party

LITTLE COOKIE HOUSES

Assorted large crackers and cookies (such as Wasa
  Crisps and Social Teas) for building, plus sugar
  wafers and round, scalloped butter cookies for
  decorating
1 batch Ornamental Frosting (see page 128) or
  1 tub (16 ounces) ready-to-use decorator icing
  (see Sources, page 156)
Assorted decorations and colorful candies,
  including pretzel sticks, ice cream cones, Necco
  wafers, Starlight mints, M&M's, gumdrops,
  Mike & Ike candy, mini Chiclets, and red hots

1. Assemble houses or other structures from large
crackers or cookies, attaching pieces with Ornamental
Frosting. (Frosting recipe makes 3 cups; you may need
more or less, depending on how houses are decorated.)
Spread frosting on cookie edges; hold edges together
for a few minutes until set. (If the party is for small
children, you may want to assemble some houses
before they arrive.)

2. Decorate as desired. For log cabin, ice outer walls
and attach pretzel sticks. For church, make steeple
from iced sugar wafer, with pretzel cross at top; make
doors from sugar wafers trimmed at top with knife.
Decorate roofs with assorted candies. For Necco wafer
shingles, spread roof generously with frosting.
Starting at bottom of roof, arrange wafers so they over-
lap slightly. Use upside-down ice cream cones for cas-
tle turrets: Spread with frosting and sprinkle with
multicolored nonpareils. Attach decorations with
Ornamental Frosting.

Gingerbread
Candyland Cottage

This festive fantasy of gingerbread, icing, and candy requires only 6 shaped pattern pieces.

MATERIALS

Gingersnap Dough (see below)
2 batches Ornamental Frosting (see page 128)
Poster board, cardboard, or foam core for patterns
    plus paper
6 disposable decorating bags
6 couplers
#2 thin writing decorating tip (1/32-inch opening)
#3 writing decorating tip (1/16-inch opening)
#25 star decorating tip (1/2-inch opening)
#65 leaf decorating tip (smallest available)
brown, red, blue, green, and black food-color pastes
nontoxic marker
1 piece (9 1/2" by 10 1/2" or larger) foam core,
    3/16 inch thick or 2 layers heavy cardboard
    glued together
1 bag (8 ounces) plain candy-coated
    chocolate candies

ROLL, CUT, AND BAKE

GINGERSNAP DOUGH

1 1/2 cups heavy or whipping cream
2 1/2 cups packed brown sugar
1 1/4 cups molasses
1 tablespoon ground ginger
1 tablespoon grated lemon peel
2 tablespoons baking soda
9 cups all-purpose flour

1. To prepare the dough: Whip cream. Add sugar, molasses, ginger, lemon peel, and baking soda. Stir 10 minutes. Add flour and work with hands until smooth. Cover and refrigerate overnight.

2. To roll dough: Roll out on greased and floured 17" by 14" cookie sheets; placing 3/16-inch or 1/8-inch dowels on either side will help you roll out dough to uniform thickness. Before cutting shapes, chill rolled dough on cookie sheets in refrigerator or freezer. Rechill as necessary to keep it "leather hard," which makes it easier to cut.

3. To make patterns: Enlarge diagrams to full size and cut patterns from poster board, heavy cardboard, or foam core.

4. To cut and bake: Flour patterns. Using pizza wheel or sharp knife, cut out cottage pieces, leaving at least 1/2 inch between them. Remove scraps (they can be rerolled, though the cookies won't be as smooth). Chill cutout pieces for 10 minutes. Brush dough with water before baking. Preheat oven to 300°F and bake 25 to 30 minutes or until firm to the touch. While gingerbread is still warm, place patterns on top again and trim shapes to match if necessary. Let cool on cookie sheets.

DECORATE

1. Windows and Door: Trace pattern pieces on paper; cut out windows and door from paper to create a stencil. Place stencil on gingerbread. Trace outline of windows and door using a nontoxic marker.

2. Roof: Using nontoxic marker, and following design on roof pattern, draw 6 rows of garland on each half of roof.

3. Make 1 batch of Ornamental Frosting and divide into 5 containers. Tint 1 dark brown, 1 red, 1 light blue, 1 green, and let 1 remain white. Decorate cottage using frosting, decorating bags, and specified tips. Be sure to cover each bowl of frosting with plastic wrap until using so it does not dry out.

4. With dark-brown frosting and #2 writing tip, outline windows, shutters, door, door hinges, and white trim on front of cottage. Pipe frosting over rows of garland on roof. Let dry.

5. Reserve 1 tablespoon red frosting. Thin the remaining red frosting with less than ½ teaspoon water until it is of spreading consistency. Check by dropping a teaspoon of frosting back into the bowl. If the dropped frosting disappears by the time you count to 10, the frosting is the right consistency. If the frosting mounds and is still visible, add a few more drops of water. Using #2 tip, fill in shutters and door with thinned red frosting. Let dry.

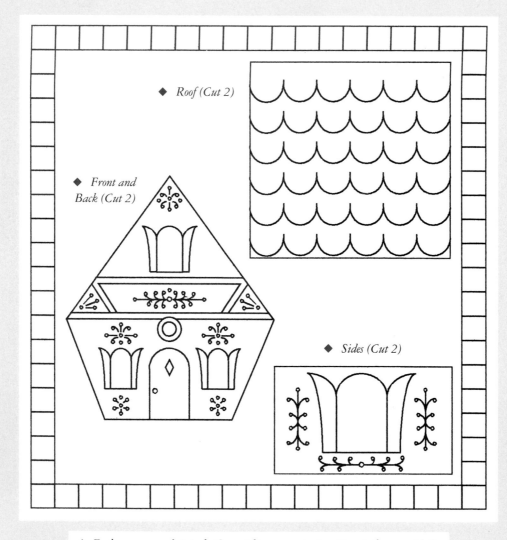

◆ *Roof (Cut 2)*

◆ *Front and Back (Cut 2)*

◆ *Sides (Cut 2)*

◆ *Each square equals 1 inch. Connect lines across pattern pieces to form a grid. Or enlarge patterns 400 percent using a copy machine.*

6. With blue frosting and #3 writing tip, pipe a row of blue dots, some big, some small, below each window and around door. Thin remaining blue frosting as in step 5. Using #2 tip, fill in windows and small window on the door. Let dry.

7. With green frosting and #3 tip, pipe green dots around tops of windows. With #65 small leaf tip, pipe wreath above door. With reserved red frosting and #2 tip, pipe red dots on wreath; make vertical lines on door.

8. Thin half of white frosting as in step 5 and using #2 tip, fill in white trim on cottage front. Let dry. Using #3 tip, pipe wavy brown design on top of white trim.

9. Using green frosting and #3 tip, pipe 3 rows of green garland on each half of roof over brown frosting. Using white frosting and #2 tip, pipe rows of white dots on roof. Let dry.

10. Mix the remaining white frosting and some of the brown frosting to make tan. Using tan frosting and #2 tip, pipe dots for center of folk-art designs above and below windows and around white trim. Then pipe teardrop shapes with green, tan, and brown frosting around the tan dots. Using tan frosting and #3 tip, pipe 3 rows of tan garland on each roof half in between rows of green garland. Attach candy-coated chocolate candies between rows of garland, using frosting. Using tan frosting and #2 tip, pipe crisscrosses on windowpanes and on door window; make doorknob.

11. Mix all remaining colors together and add a little black food-color paste. Using #2 tip, pipe vertical lines on shutters and hinges on door. Let all pieces dry overnight before assembling.

ASSEMBLE

1. Make the second batch of Ornamental Frosting. Using #25 star tip, pipe a thick band of frosting on the bottom and side edges of the front piece. Place it upright on the foam core (position it so cottage will be centered on foam core). Ice edges of the 2 side pieces and attach to front. (Carefully place heavy cans against pieces to support structure while you work.)

◆ *Here, simply decorated gingerbread snowflakes are strung with raffia for natural, homespun charm.*

Ice edges of cottage back and attach to sides. Let dry for a few hours.

2. Using #25 star tip, pipe frosting along top edge of cottage and top of roof pieces. Place roof pieces on cottage; hold or prop up until frosting sets. With a dab of frosting on each, attach candy-coated chocolate candies in rows along roof peak and down diagonal roof edges; pipe dots of green frosting between candy-coated chocolate candies.

3. Cover exposed foam core with white frosting to resemble snow. Make cobblestone path in front of door: Using #3 tip and remaining dark frosting, pipe unmatched dots to resemble cobblestones. Pipe a row of small uniform dots along exposed wall seams.

Sources

Children's Pajamas

AFTER THE STORK catalog
(800) 859-8167 TO REQUEST A CATALOG

Craft Supplies

CARDINAL INTERNATIONAL, INC.
(Octine Arcoroc salad plate)
P.O. BOX 466
WAYNE, NJ 07470 FOR A LOCAL SUPPLIER

PLAID ENTERPRISES, INC.
1649 INTERNATIONAL COURT
NORCROSS, GA 30093
(800) 842-4197 FOR A LOCAL SUPPLIER

Baking Supplies

DUPONT TEFLON NONSTICK BAKEWARE LINERS
(800) 986-2857 FOR A LOCAL SUPPLIER

WILTON ENTERPRISES
(meringue powder; ready-to-use decorator icing)
(708) 963-7100 EXT. 320 TO ORDER

Good Housekeeping METRIC CONVERSION CHART

VOLUME

1 teaspoon	5 ml
1 tablespoon	15 ml
¼ cup	60 ml
⅓ cup	80 ml
½ cup	120 ml
⅔ cup	160 ml
¾ cup	180 ml
1 cup	240 ml
1 pint (U.S.)	475 ml
1 quart	.95 liter
1 quart plus ¼ cup	1 liter
1 gallon (U.S.)	3.8 liters

TEMPERATURE

(To convert from Fahrenheit to Celsius: subtract 32, multiply by 5, then divide by 9.)

32°F	0°C
212°F	100°C
250°F	121°C
325°F	163°C
350°F	176°C
375°F	190°C
400°F	205°C
425°F	218°C
450°F	232°C

WEIGHT

1 ounce	28.3 grams
4 ounces	113 grams
8 ounces	227 grams
12 ounces	340.2 grams
1 pound	.45 kilo
2 pounds, 3¼ ounces	1 kilo (1,000 grams)

ACKNOWLEDGMENTS *and* CREDITS

ACKNOWLEDGMENTS

Octine Arcoroc Salad Plate: Courtesy of Cardinal International, Inc.

CREDITS

Photo Credits

Peter Ardito: pages 123, 126

Mary Ellen Bartley: page 121

Augustus Butera: pages 34, 35

Brian Hagiwara: front cover, Gingerbread Candyland Cottage; pages 65, 73, 76, 77, 90, 93, 97 to 103, 112, 118, 153

John Kane: pages 22 (right) to 24, 46, 47, 52 (Ribbon and Card Garland), 53, 54, 55, 155, 157

Kevin Lein: front cover, Christmas Stockings; 26, 27, 30-31, 37

Michael Luppino: pages 12, 44, 45

Peter Margonelli: pages 6-7, 13

Keith Scott Morton: front cover, Wreath; back cover, Floral and Candle Centerpiece, Tree, Sugared Fruit; front flap; pages 1 to 5, 9 to 11, 14 to 22 (left), 25, 28, 29, 36, 38 to 43, 48 to 51, 52 (paper snowflakes, right), 56, 156, 159, 160

David Murray and Jules Selmes: pages 60, 62

Steven Mark Needham: pages 59, 63, 66

Alan Richardson: back cover, Austrian Drum Torte; pages 95, 105, 109, 111, 115, 116, 150, 151

Ann Stratton: page 69

Mark Thomas: front cover, Cookies; back flap; pages 75, 78 to 88, 91, 129 to 148

Photo Styling (Commissioned photographs)

Richard Kollath: pages 1, 2, 4, 5, 9, 10, 11, 14, 15, 16, 17, 18, 19, 20, 21, 22 (left), 25, 28, 29, 36, 38, 39, 40, 41, 43 (step-by-step photos, left), 48, 49, 50, 51, 52 (paper snowflakes, right), 56

Matthew Mead: pages 12, 44, 45

Designers

Richard Kollath: Silver Wreath, page 1; Berries in Silver Horn, page 2; Silver Tree, pages 4-5; Dried Florals in Basket, page 10; Roses in Ice Skate, page 11; Terra-Cotta-Potted Trees, page 15; Tabletop Topiaries, page 16; Static Wreath, Pepper Berry Double Wreath, Mixed Greens Wreath, Moss-Lichen Wreath, pages 18-22; Pomanders, page 25; Sugared Fruit, page 28; Tree, page 38; Ornaments, pages 40-41; Luminaria, pages 44-45; Floral and Candle Centerpiece, page 48; Cranberry Floral Centerpiece, page 49; Hurricane Lamp Floral Centerpiece, page 50; Gilded Pear Place Marker, page 56.

Karin Lidbeck: Golden Acorn Wreath, page 22; Birch Bark Cornucopia, page 23; Pomanders on Tree, page 24; Little Angels Pajamas, pages 34-35; Kissing Balls, pages 42-43; Cinnamon Stick and Candle Centerpiece, Garland-Wrapped Lamppost, pages 46-47; Ribbon and Card Garland, page 52; Ribbon and Paper Snowflake Tree, page 53; Window Swags, page 54; Gift-Wrapped Pillow, Button Wreath, page 55; Gingerbread Snowflake Cookies, page 155.

Matthew Mead: Christmas Stockings, page 30; Découpage Plate, page 36

Cookie Recipe Credits

The following cookie recipes first appeared in the December 1996 issue of Good Housekeeping *as winners of a contest announced and promoted in* Good Housekeeping*. The recipes have been adapted and tested by the* Good Housekeeping *Test Kitchen.*

Page 128: Great-Granny's Old-Time Spice Cookies, Shirley A. Fisher, Bethlehem, PA. Page 130: Sand Tarts, Vivian A. Eck, Williamsport, PA; Jelly Centers, Ann Marie Reinle, Massapequa, NY. Page 131: Layered Date Bars, Mary Beth Rollick, Munroe Falls, OH. Page 132: Aunt Tess's Anisette Cookies, Ann Cullen, Wantagh, NY. Page 133: Pennsylvania-Dutch Brownies, Yvonne D. Kanoff, Mount Joy, PA; Miss Elsie's Almond Slices, Ann Wood, Columbia, MD. Page 135: Mom's Pfeffernusse, Carol A. Buck, Sherman Oaks, CA; Christmas Rocks, Betty Pfeifer, Bay Village, OH. Page 136: Honey Cookies, Dawn Zimmerman, Couderay, WI; Peanutty Yummy Bars, Susanne Corker, Lake Orion, MI. Page 137: Colorful Holiday Cookies, Loretta Rakofsky, Dallas, TX. Page 138: Sally Ann Cookies, Sue Riesterer, Manitowoc, WI. Page 139: Finska Kakor, Sue Larraway, Sunnyvale, CA. Page 141: Noisettines, Laurence Mancini Ilanjian, Taconic, CT; Horns, Helen McGrath, Camarillo, CA. Page 142: Greek Cinnamon Paximadia, Kathryn Marie Petrofanis, San Pedro, CA; Vinegar Cookies, Winifred Bissonnette, Ludlow, VT. Page 145: Chocolate Sambuca Cookies, Leslie R. Husted, Clinton, NY; Czechoslovakian Cookies, Barbara Karpinski, Somerset, NJ. Page 146: Hazelnut Cookies, Susan Willey Spalt, Carrboro, NC; Wooden-Spoon Cookies, Cindie David, Lawrenceville, GA. Page 147: Ricotta-Cheese Cookies, Naoma R. Felt, Bradenton, FL. Page 149: Cinnamon Twists, Carrie Deegan, Glen Cove, NY; Greek Christmas Cookies, Diane Sanchez, Auburndale, FL.

INDEX